# Cambridge Elements ☰

**Elements in Ethics**
edited by
Ben Eggleston
*University of Kansas*
Dale E. Miller
*Old Dominion University, Virginia*

# KANT'S ETHICS

Kate A. Moran
*Brandeis University*

CAMBRIDGE
UNIVERSITY PRESS

# CAMBRIDGE
## UNIVERSITY PRESS

University Printing House, Cambridge CB2 8BS, United Kingdom

One Liberty Plaza, 20th Floor, New York, NY 10006, USA

477 Williamstown Road, Port Melbourne, VIC 3207, Australia

314–321, 3rd Floor, Plot 3, Splendor Forum, Jasola District Centre,
New Delhi – 110025, India

103 Penang Road, #05–06/07, Visioncrest Commercial, Singapore 238467

Cambridge University Press is part of the University of Cambridge.

It furthers the University's mission by disseminating knowledge in the pursuit of
education, learning, and research at the highest international levels of excellence.

www.cambridge.org
Information on this title: www.cambridge.org/9781108718943
DOI: 10.1017/9781108754637

First published 2022

*A catalogue record for this publication is available from the British Library.*

ISBN 978-1-108-71894-3 Paperback
ISSN 2516-4031 (online)
ISSN 2516-4023 (print)

# Kant's Ethics

Elements in Ethics

DOI: 10.1017/9781108754637
First published online: February 2022

Kate A. Moran
*Brandeis University*

**Author for correspondence:** Kate A. Moran, kmoran@brandeis.edu

**Abstract:** This Element provides an overview of Immanuel Kant's arguments regarding the content of the moral law (the categorical imperative), as well as an exposition of his arguments for the bindingness of the moral law for rational agents. It also considers common objections to Kant's ethics.

**Keywords:** Immanuel Kant, categorical imperative, moral law, autonomy, ethics

ISBNs: 9781108718943 (PB), 9781108754637 (OC)
ISSNs: 2516-4031 (online), 2516-4023 (print)

# Contents

# 1 Introduction

## 1.1 Why Study Kantian Ethics?

Readers and students of Kant's ethics sometimes face a frustrating paradox. On the one hand, Kant's moral theory seems to describe a moral principle that is, on its surface, almost intuitive. Familiar themes of reciprocity, impartiality, and fairness play a central role, and one is left, perhaps, with the sense that the moral code described is, at the end of the day, something not too far removed from the golden rule or some similar preschool edict. On the other hand, as soon as one begins to study the theory carefully, one is beset with difficulty. Kant's argumentation is technical and dense, and it takes a puzzling path through intricate analyses of intentional action and moral judgment just to arrive at a statement of the moral law that is itself difficult to unpack and apply in every case – a moral law that apparently contains several different versions or formulations within itself. All of this is to say nothing of the exactitude and strenuousness with which we are apparently supposed to live our moral lives and the unwavering devotion one ought to have to morality itself. After all of that, a person could be forgiven for wondering if she might not be better off just sticking with the moral code she learned in preschool, after all.

The Kantian reply is straightforward: the moral code you learned from your preschool teachers or parents, though it has perhaps served you well, came from an external authority, not from you. True, there might be a sense in which you sometimes endorse it or parts of it, but you were not its legislator, and this makes all the difference. What is more, there is (if we're honest) a puzzle about *why* you follow it at all, if and when you do. Maybe you have simply internalized the authority that your teachers and parents had over you so long ago. Or maybe you discovered along the way that following these general rules was the best way to avoid trouble, get by, or bring about your own well-being or that of those you care most about. But then what about those times when – as so often happens – it doesn't actually succeed in accomplishing these ends? Many a former preschool student has wondered, in later years, what the point of following all these rules is when the ones who flaunt them or treat them as mere fiction seem to get so much further ahead.

What Kant's moral theory has to offer is a way to make sense of our moral obligations from the ground up, as it were. Kant offers an account of morality whose validity does not depend on external authority, or on the positive consequences it might bring to oneself or others. It is a morality that each of us authors herself, in light of certain rational requirements and in light of the fact that we share a moral community with other agents. The aim of this text is to provide an overview of this moral principle, including its foundations and application.

## 1.2 Overview of the Text

The text begins with a survey of some of the major themes that run throughout Kant's moral philosophy. These, I hope, will provide some guidance and context as the text moves on to a study of Kant's arguments concerning the foundations of morality. Although the text serves as an introduction to the arguments that Kant provides regarding the moral law, it is not a commentary on the text that many students read when first studying Kant's moral philosophy, the *Groundwork for the Metaphysics of Morals* (*Groundwork*).[1] Nevertheless, the section headings in this text should provide some guidance with regard to where overlap does occur.

The text continues with a discussion of Kant's account of moral and nonmoral willing (Section 3), which is central to his overall argument. It moves from there to a discussion of the first two formulations of the categorical imperative: the formula of universal law and the formula of humanity (Sections 4 and 5, respectively).[2] The text then discusses Kant's account of moral motivation (Section 6), which leads naturally to a discussion of autonomy and freedom of the will (Sections 7 and 8, respectively). In Section 9, I attempt to answer a few of the more common objections to Kantian ethics.

I have tried, as far as possible, to avoid jargon in an effort to make the text accessible to a wide range of readers. Nevertheless, Kant's argumentation can often be difficult, no matter how straightforwardly one tries to present it, and one Kantian argument can often admit several plausible interpretations. Alas, a text like this cannot do justice to the various interpretations and arguments that Kant scholars have offered over the years, though I have attempted to highlight moments in the discussion where there is considerable debate among Kant scholars. Footnotes throughout the text also provide guidance for readers interested in pursuing a topic in more detail.

## 2 Themes in Kantian Ethics

### 2.1 Universality and Necessity

Universality and necessity are central concepts throughout Kant's philosophical system. In his moral philosophy, they play a crucial role as part of his argument

---

[1] Commentaries on *Groundwork* certainly exist (see Allison, 2011; Guyer, 2007; Timmermann, 2007). Uleman (2010) and Wood (1999) offer useful commentaries on Kant's ethical thought as a whole.

[2] Among Kant scholars, there is some variation in how the various formulations of the categorical imperative are counted and categorized. For example, Paton (1971) takes the formula of the law of nature to be a version of the formula of universal law and the formulations of autonomy and the realm of ends as falling under the formula of humanity. Timmermann (2007) presents the formula of universal law as the overarching formulation, of which the others are subspecies.

about the nature of moral laws and moral obligation. Among Kant's foundational premises is a definitional point – that a moral law, if it is truly a *law*, must hold universally and necessarily (*GMS*, 4:389). Kant takes this to be uncontroversial, and his argumentative strategy will be to investigate what kind of moral code could possibly have these features of universality and necessity. Ultimately, he will conclude that only the principle of morality that he calls the categorical imperative can fit this description. Relatedly, our obligation to abide by the moral law described by the categorical imperative is also universal and necessary. In other words, the categorical imperative describes the content of a moral law that all rational agents are bound by necessarily. The moral law is thus necessary and universal both in the content that it describes and in its account of agents' moral obligation. A large part of Kant's argument – and the discussion in this text – will be devoted to arguing for these claims.

Perhaps because of Kant's insistence upon universality and necessity with respect to the obligation it imposes, he is sometimes cast as a kind of unwavering rule fetishist, most infamously in examples like those concerning the "murderer at the door," in which an agent is faced with a choice of whether to unwaveringly follow a rule (e.g. against lying) or break it in order to save a friend's life or for the sake of some other worthy goal. It would be an exaggeration to say that this impression is entirely unfounded, and there is no simple or straightforward way to respond to these objections and counterexamples.[3] Still, the objection gets a good deal of extra steam from the assumption that Kant is offering a fixed system of preexisting commandments or rules. However, Kant's moral system is not, despite its insistence upon necessity, a system of *rules*. Instead, Kant sets out a test of *permissibility*: The categorical imperative tests whether the principle or plan of action that one has set out for oneself is permissible or impermissible. Now, of course, certain types of principles – those that involve the subjugation of others, for example – will turn out to be impermissible whatever the circumstance. Still, it is central to Kant's account that the agent considers her own proposed principle of action and whether this would be permissible. Kant's moral system, though at times rigorous and demanding, does not describe a moral world in which obligation is imposed upon agents as a set of commandments from a stern and unforgiving external authority. Instead, Kant thinks that morality can only be imposed on an agent from within. It is and must be self-given. This is Kant's notion of autonomy.

---

[3] For a detailed discussion on the question of the murderer at the door, especially regarding how to understand the notion of a lie, see Mahon, 2003, 2009.

## 2.2 Autonomy

Often, we use the term "autonomy" to describe self-sufficiency or self-determination, as when we discuss patient autonomy in healthcare settings or the importance of developing children's sense of autonomy in the context of early education. For Kant, the term has a much narrower meaning: it refers to an agent's capacity to simultaneously be subject to and the legislator of the moral law. On the Kantian view, in other words, it is crucial that agents are the source of the moral prescription that they themselves follow. This does not mean, however, that agents can arbitrarily decide upon the content of the law. As Kant puts it, the agent is the author of the "obligation in accordance with the law" but not of the law itself (*MS*, 6:227).

This view sets Kant's theory apart from theories according to which a moral code is given and enforced by an external authority, whether this is a divine authority or some other, worldly authority. But it also sets Kant apart from philosophers who argue that moral knowledge and moral motivation stem from an emotive response or moral sense.[4] Although that sort of moral sense would be "internal" to the agent, Kant argues that this does not put the agent in charge any more than she is in charge of any other impulse or feeling – say, of her hunger or her sadness. This brings us to a key point about autonomy – in order to be the author of the law, an agent's *reason*, not her feelings or her desires, must be legislative.[5]

Importantly, however, autonomy does not mean that the moral law is arbitrary or "up to us" in the sense that each individual can simply decide the difference between right and wrong on the basis of what is convenient or brings her the most pleasure, for example. That would be to make morality a matter of instrumental reason, that is, of reasoning about which actions best promote one's interest. Reason plays an important role in Kant's ethics, but it is not *instrumental* reason that plays this role. Crucial to his account of autonomy – and morality in general – is Kant's view that moral agents are capable of another type of reason altogether – a type of reason that is able to consider whether our actions are moral, without thinking about whether they are in our own interest. Now, of course, these two types of reason often find themselves at odds with one another; the most prudent course of action from a self-interested perspective is not always (alas!) the right action, considered morally. This, too, will be a theme in Kant's ethics: we are all too aware of the fact that doing the right thing can often involve a degree of pain or sacrifice. But the very fact that we recognize

---

[4] Kant has in mind moral sense theorists, for example, Shaftesbury, Hutcheson, and Hume.

[5] Reason is legislative in the sense that it issues the moral principle to be followed. Moral motivation, for Kant, is a trickier subject. See Section 6 for further discussion.

this tension, Kant would say, gives us a clue that we are capable of recognizing constraints on our actions whose source is something other than self-interest.

## 2.3 Egalitarianism and Impartiality

The discussion that follows will often emphasize Kant's egalitarian commitments. At the root of these is Kant's conviction that every rational agent is an end in herself and should never be treated as a mere means to an end (see Section 5). This gives all rational agents a kind of dignity that can never be exchanged or traded for the sake of other ends (*GMS*, 4:435). This commitment to the fundamental, inalienable dignity of all rational agents means that Kant's egalitarian commitments can often be stated as prohibitions against making an exception for oneself or using others merely as a means toward one's own ends. Kant is thus in some sense the forerunner of contemporary theories that emphasize treating others in ways that they could rationally consent to from an impartial standpoint or treating others in ways that they could not reasonably reject.[6] Crucially absent from Kant's egalitarianism is the approach taken by many consequentialist theories, according to which each relevant individual has one "vote," as it were, when it comes to deciding which available course of action will bring about the most net utility. Indeed, this approach easily violates the prohibitions described above, since on this account, one person's dignity may sometimes need to be sacrificed for the sake of the greater good.[7]

## 2.4 Freedom and Nature

Finally, it is important to note that on the Kantian view, we are both moral beings and sensible beings. This means that we are capable of understanding and giving ourselves the moral law *and* that we are simultaneously subject to feelings of pleasure and displeasure and the desires and inclinations that develop from these feelings. We occupy, as it were, two different worlds and find ourselves continuously navigating between them. This has several important implications for Kant's ethics as a whole. First, it will mean that we will experience morality as a kind of obligation or constraint. Though self-imposed, morality will nevertheless tell us that some of the things we plan or hope to do on the basis of inclination are impermissible. This brings us to a second point: moral life, for sensible creatures like us, will involve a host of different feelings; when we discover that a proposed plan of action is impermissible, we experience a kind of "pain" or even "humiliation" (*KpV*, 5:74). This, in turn, inspires a feeling of awe or reverence for the moral law (*KpV*, 5:74). Thus, although

---

[6] See, for example, Rawls, 1980; Scanlon, 1998.
[7] See especially Rawls, 1971, p. 24, (rev. ed.) on this point.

feeling cannot serve as the *foundation* for a universal and necessary principle of morality, Kant's account of the moral existence of sensible yet rational creatures includes a good deal of feeling indeed.

We are sensible beings, and we are also finite beings. We have desires and ends we cannot always accomplish on our own, and we often need the assistance of others, whether this is because we want to learn a skill or because we suffer and need help. The fact that we are sensible and finite beings will thus also serve as an important premise in Kant's arguments regarding our duties of assistance toward others. Taken together, the preceding observations indicate that our sensible nature can often be the source of need or frustration. Although Kant sometimes suggests that the best or most rational thing would be to wish to be free from inclination altogether (*GMS*, 4:454), he does not, in my view, mean to renounce our sensible nature altogether. In the first place, it would be an idle wish. Furthermore, however, it is because we are sensible that we can take disinterested pleasure in beauty and experience happiness when our interests are fulfilled. Kant is not a Stoic: he thinks that our general well-being – which he would term "happiness," though the Stoics would not – is important to us; it is a conditional good (i.e. it is good as long as it is consistent with morality). Rather than seeking to renounce our sensible nature, then, Kant is best understood as seeking a way to make happiness consistent with virtue, as far as this is possible.[8]

## 3 The Moral Law and the Will

Having considered some of the major themes in Kant's ethics, we are now in a position to examine Kant's foundational arguments regarding the moral law and moral willing. Kant sets out by posing a question: If there is such a thing as a universally valid moral law, what would be the characteristics of that law? A further question follows immediately: Given the characteristics of a universally valid moral law, what characteristics must moral *agents* have? Specifically, how should we describe the will of the agent who is bound by this law? For sake of exposition, we will discuss these questions independently of one another, but there is an important sense in which they are intimately connected in Kant's arguments regarding morality. In particular, Kant's arguments regarding the content of morality are only provisional until he can also demonstrate that moral agents are actually capable of and subject to the moral law that he describes.[9]

---

[8] Kant seeks to accomplish this, in large part, via his account of the so-called "highest (derived) good," discussed briefly in Section 9 of this text.

[9] This is the structure of the argument in the *Groundwork of the Metaphysics of Morals*. See Section 8 for more detail about the argument and how it shifts over time.

Kant takes it as a foundational starting premise that a moral law must hold with unconditional necessity. This is a general, definitional point about the characteristics of a *law*: If something is to count as a *law* – and not merely as a guideline, for instance – it must be the kind of principle that applies universally (*GMS*, 4:389). Kant thus takes the necessary character of the moral law to be contained within the notion of lawfulness. Hence, insofar as we are looking for a description of the moral *law*, then, we are looking for an account of morality that is able to account for this universality. As we will see in what follows, Kant thinks that this rules out many of the more popular contending accounts of morality.

The moral law – if indeed there is such a thing – applies universally and necessarily. But to *whom* does it apply necessarily? We shouldn't assume, for example, that because it is universal and necessary, the moral law applies to all living creatures, all sentient creatures, or even all creatures with only limited rational capacities. While we might think that nonhuman animals deserve some type of moral consideration, we tend not to think of our pets, for example, as fellow moral agents capable of recognizing and following moral guidelines.[10] This is why many, if not most, of us find it perfectly acceptable to manage and condition our pets' behavior by putting them in kennels or on leashes and not with appeals to their sense of fairness or reciprocity. Insofar as there is a universally valid moral law, Kant will argue that the beings it applies to will have to have the capacity to recognize laws or principles and to let their action be guided by those laws or principles. In Kant's terminology, the moral law applies to agents who are able to "act according to the representation of a law" (*GMS*, 4:412). Any creature that is capable of acting according to the representation of a law is, in theory, capable of morality and subject to its requirements. Kant's notion of acting under the representation of a law is central to his account of action in general – that is, to his account of both moral action and nonmoral action. It will thus be helpful to examine this capacity in more detail.

Any instance of intentional action involves, in the Kantian terminology, an *objective determining ground* and a *subjective determining ground*. The objective determining ground is the guideline, principle, or law that the will follows, depending on its aims and circumstances (e.g. *GMS*, 4:400). The subjective determining ground provides the motivation for the will (e.g. *GMS*, 4:413n).[11]

---

[10] For further discussion of Kant's arguments regarding our duties concerning nonhuman animals, see Kain, 2010; Timmermann, 2005; and Varden, 2020. A novel Kantian account is offered in Korsgaard, 2018.

[11] The subjective determining ground is thus not the same as a "maxim," which Kant describes as a "subjective principle of willing" (*GMS*, 4:400n). Rather, it is what moves an agent to adopt a maxim.

To get a clearer grasp on how objective and subjective determinations of the will work in concert, it may be useful to begin with an example of nonmoral willing. Imagine a dressmaker who wants to make a strapless dress. She knows that in order to do this, she will need to add structure to the bodice of the dress, say, by inserting boning. Here, the objective principle informing the dressmaker's choice of action is something like: "In order to make a strapless dress, you need to add boning to the bodice." The objective principle is objective because it applies to any dressmaker who aims to make a strapless dress. Still, although the principle is objective, it is not authoritative or action-guiding for every agent, for the simple reason that only a very small subset of agents is, at any given moment, concerned with making a strapless dress. In order for this particular objective principle to apply to an agent, she must have the relevant aim or end. The desire to make a strapless dress is the subjective determining ground of the agent's will. Now, we can see how objective and subjective determining grounds work together in the case of nonmoral willing: the objective determining ground provides principles that any agent with a particular subjective determining ground should follow in order to accomplish her ends.

Notice that in the nonmoral case, neither the objective nor the subjective determining ground of the will is universally and necessarily valid. This is probably easier to see in the case of the subjective determining ground: the principles that describe dressmaking will do nothing to move the agent hard at work building a chest of drawers or filing her taxes. But even the objective principles that apply to agents who *do* adopt certain ends are changeable: facts about the agent and the world can affect the objective principle that guides an agent's choice of action. Before the advent of various textile innovations like elastic, boning might have been essential to the construction of a strapless dress. Today, such innovations provide other options, and this changes the objective principle a person must follow when she sets out to design such a garment.

It is worth pausing here to note that this contingency regarding objective principles is not just a feature of textile design or other "imperatives of skill," as Kant will call them (*GMS*, 4:415). It is also a feature of more general aims and projects, most notably our pursuit of happiness. Many of our actions aim at happiness, but it is impossible to pin down an objective principle that will invariably lead to the attainment of happiness. This is because agents and the world they live in are unpredictable and constantly changing. A principle of saving money for later in life is perhaps a good general objective principle of happiness, but not if one's life is cut short unexpectedly. In that case, it might have been better from the point of view of happiness to spend one's money while one had the opportunity. And it is not at all uncommon to find that some of the things that we think will bring us happiness ultimately fall short in this regard, sometimes because we ourselves change over time. These observations about the variability and unpredictability of any objective principle regarding happiness lead Kant to reject the idea that the pursuit of happiness – that of our own or that of general happiness – could be the foundation of a moral *law* (*GMS*, 4:418). Kant acknowledges that we do, in fact, all pursue happiness as an end, but the principles guiding its attainment are themselves far from necessary or universal. Of course, even if the attainment of happiness were predictable and determinate, it still could not serve as a foundational for the moral law, since each of us only seeks our *own* happiness. The harmony and universality required by a moral *law* would be thrown into chaos by a principle founded on *general* happiness (*KpV*, 5:28).

In Kant's view, *any* kind of intentional action requires subjective and objective determining grounds. So far, our examples have only concerned nonmoral action, which operates according to subjective and objective determinations of the will that are contingent upon facts about the world or upon the aims and desires of particular agents. But *moral* willing is also a kind of willing, and it must have its own objective and subjective determining grounds. As we have already noted, Kant thinks that a moral law applies necessarily. So we can think of Kant's project – particularly in the *Groundwork of the Metaphysics of Morals* and the *Critique of Practical Reason* – as a search for and explication of the objective and subjective determining grounds of the will when it engages in *moral* willing. The aim, in other words, is to find objective and subjective determining grounds of the will that could carry with them absolute necessity and universality.

But here we run into a serious challenge. We can readily locate determining grounds of the will for nonmoral willing precisely because facts about the world and agents' aims make these clear to us. Facts about gravity, the shape of the human body, and the physical properties of fabric combine to generate a rule about how to construct a strapless dress. Note, however, that it is precisely these facts about the world that make the principle contingent. Similarly, a person's desire to make a strapless dress explains immediately and straightforwardly why she is following the principle to insert boning into a dress. But, again, the desire to make a strapless dress is a contingent matter – indeed, partially contingent on what is fashionable in any given context! Thus, the very same features of the world and agents' desires that make nonmoral action relatively easy to explain also *exclude* them from consideration as the basis of necessary and universal *moral* willing. In order to find objective and subjective determinations of the will for moral willing, we will thus have to look elsewhere.

## 4 The Moral Law: The Formula of Universal Law

We are now in a position to consider Kant's explication of the moral law – the principle, or objective determining ground of the will when the will is guided by morality, as opposed to inclination and desire. Above, we saw that in the nonmoral case, agents' aims, combined with empirical facts about the world, generate the rules that agents use to guide their actions. But morality must apply universally and necessarily, and agents' aims and empirical facts about the world are wholly contingent matters.[12] So we seem to be at an impasse, since everything that typically provides content to the rules or laws that a will acts upon is excluded by virtue of its contingency. However, Kant argues that one thing still remains even after we have abstracted any material aim: something we might call the form of lawfulness as such. As he puts it, "Since I have robbed the will of all impulses that could arise for it from following some particular law, nothing remains but as such the universal conformity of actions with law, which alone is to serve the will as its principle" (*GMS*, 4:402).

Stated in these terms, Kant's thinking is perhaps a bit murky. It may be helpful to think of Kant as saying something like the following: "Since everything that normally ties rules or laws to the will is excluded as contingent in the case of morality, the only thing left is to see whether the very notion of a necessary and universal law might *itself* give content to a moral law."[13] And Kant thinks it does: the principle that emerges, he argues, is the following: "I ought never to proceed except in such a way *that I could also will that my maxim should become a universal law*" (*GMS*, 4:402, emphasis in original). This is Kant's famous categorical imperative. It is an *imperative* in the sense that it is an action-guiding, objective determining ground of the will, and it is *categorical* because it applies necessarily and universally to any agent capable of acting under the representation of a law or principle, no matter their particular aims or interests.

It is worth keeping a few things in mind at this stage of Kant's argument. First, at this stage in the *Groundwork*, Kant is not yet arguing that this moral law "exists" or that it actually applies to us. That will require more argument (see Section 8). Here, Kant's only assertion is that *if there is a moral law*, it would have to have these characteristics. Imagine, by way of outlandish example,

---

[12] Terminologically, Kant thus often distinguishes between a *rule*, which can admit of variation and contingency, and a *law*, which cannot. However, he does not always abide by this distinction.

[13] It bears pointing out that some scholars have worried about a gap in Kant's argument at this stage. See, for example, Allison, 1996 and Aune, 1980. Korsgaard (1996, pp. 61–64) offers a reconstruction of Kant's argument. Timmermann (2007) argues that the gap can be closed. See also Gaut and Kerstein, 1999.

a biologist being asked what kind of physical characteristics a unicorn would have to have in order to support such a long and heavy horn. She might be able to comment on the structure of the hypothetical unicorn's musculature without thereby committing herself to the existence of unicorns. Kant is doing something similar at this stage in the argument – he is merely arguing that if there is a moral law, then, as necessary and universal, it would have to have a particular form. We can see Kant making a similar point in the opening lines of section one the *Groundwork*, where he discusses the nature of a so-called good will. Crucially, he is not yet trying to show that such a law actually exists.[14]

Second, it is also helpful to keep in mind that the principle of morality functions differently than the empirical principles considered previously. Rather than being a statement about the sorts of actions that one ought to perform in order to bring about a desired end, it is a negative statement about the kinds of principles that one ought to *avoid*. In a sense, this is not surprising: because the principle doesn't aim at any particular end, it cannot give advice about how to accomplish that end. The principle can, at best, tell an agent how to *avoid* a certain condition, which we might for the purposes of exposition call "lawlessness." The result is that Kant's statement of the moral law is not a dogmatic assertion of a general rule (e.g. "aim to maximize general happiness") or even a set of particular rules ("don't lie," "don't cheat," "respect your elders," etc.). Rather, it describes a test of sorts that one can apply to one's proposed actions in order to see whether they are in conformity with morality or "universalizable." Kant's moral law, in other words, is a test of the *permissibility* of one's principles or maxims. This distinguishes Kant in an important way from consequentialist theories, for example, that seek to bring about or maximize a certain value or outcome.

It is important to keep in mind that the Kantian moral principle is a test of permissibility, since this will reconfigure the typical conceptual space of moral action and obligation in important ways. For a consequentialist theory, there is usually one imperative – namely, to promote or maximize some value. Insofar as one fails to intend to do this, one falls short morally. This is the source of what Bernard Williams calls "negative responsibility" – the notion that one could be morally responsible for what one fails to do, since this, too, can negatively affect outcomes (Williams, 1973). But notice that because Kant's principle describes a test of permissibility, the moral landscape changes rather drastically. One can, to be sure, choose an action that is impermissible. That would be morally wrong. But among the actions that are permissible are those that we might describe as,

---

[14] The example should not be taken too far: morality is never *really* in doubt for Kant at this stage in the argument. Still, it is helpful to keep in mind the limitations of the argument being offered.

all things being equal, neutral (watching a movie) and those that we might describe as virtuous (volunteering one's time at a local school). As we will see in what follows (Sections 4 and 5), Kant has a way to account for the difference without also committing himself to the view that one is failing or falling short morally if one does not perform as many virtuous actions as possible.

## 4.1 The Universalizability Test

The categorical imperative is a test of permissibility, but how does this test of permissibility work? The example that Kant first uses in the *Groundwork* to demonstrate this principle is that of a person who asks himself if it would be morally permissible to promise to repay a loan with no intention of repaying it, in order to acquire some money. As we will see in what follows, Kant thinks that the formula of universal law clearly rules this plan of action to be impermissible. Let us examine the features of the example and Kant's argument in more detail.

It will be helpful at this stage to introduce a bit of Kantian terminology – that of a *maxim of action*. A maxim, in Kantian terms, is a freely chosen principle, formulated as a result of prudential deliberation, that offers a statement regarding one's plan of action. In particular, it describes the end or goal that a person hopes to achieve, along with the means she intends to use to achieve that end. In the text of the *Groundwork*, maxims typically have the structure, "In circumstances C, I will perform action A in order to achieve end E."[15] In the example cited previously, the end of the agent's maxim is to acquire money, and his plan to accomplish this end is to make a false promise in the hopes of tricking his subject into handing over some money. The universalizability test is a test of an agent's *maxims*. For the test to work, it is crucial that maxims be described as including both the end and the plan of action, since the universalizability test will ultimately seek to determine whether there is a kind of contradiction involving a person's proposed plan of action and the end that she hopes to achieve.

As a test of permissibility, the categorical imperative cannot operate in a vacuum. It needs something to test, and this, again, will be the agent's maxims. More precisely, the categorical imperative requires the input of maxims that agents form on the basis of prudential deliberation. The agent in Kant's example forms his maxim to make a false promise because he has a desire or inclination for money – and, we might add, he is *disinclined* to acquire money via honest labor or asking for a favor. There is an important sense, then, in which inclinations always have the first move in Kant's analysis of moral deliberation. Inclinations suggest ends to us as agents, and it is on the basis of these ends

---

[15] Following the account of maxims in O'Neill, 1975.

that we devise maxims regarding how we might accomplish these ends. Only at that stage does the categorical imperative step in to make a ruling regarding the permissibility of these maxims.[16]

The formula of universal law tests whether an agent's maxim of action passes a test of universalizability. Now, it is important to be clear about what this means. First, what Kant does *not* have in mind: when we consider whether a proposed maxim is universalizable, we are *not* asking whether the consequences of universalizing the maxim would be valuable and then rendering a judgment on those consequences. So, for example, we might ask ourselves if it would be permissible to leave garbage behind after a picnic in the park and correctly judge that if everyone littered in the neighborhood park, it would lose its charm and be an unpleasant place to visit. But this is just to extrapolate the consequences of one's actions if they were generalized. To argue in this vein would simply be to provide a version of a (rule) consequentialist argument, since any moral judgment would still ultimately rely on an independent normative judgment about the value of a charming park as compared to the disvalue of a dirty, neglected one. But, as we have seen, Kant's moral principle does not begin with an account of some value or good that ought to be brought about or maximized.[17] This is an important point to emphasize; even some of Kant's earliest critics have trouble understanding this feature of Kant's view.[18]

Instead, the formula of universal law asks us to consider whether our maxim is consistent with the universalized version of itself. In other words, it asks us to consider whether we would run into a contradiction if we tried to act on our stated maxim if everyone else also had the same maxim. Consider again the maxim: "*In order to get some money when I need it, I will promise a friend to repay a loan with no intention to repay it.*" Would a maxim to make a false promise in order to make some easy money be consistent with the universalized version of itself? It would not, since in order for the maxim to be effective – that is, in order for the plan of action ("make a false promise") to bring about the end ("acquire some money") – the person to whom one is making the false promise needs to *believe* that the loan will be repaid. Presumably, if she were willing simply to give the money as a gift, there would be no need for the false promise in the first place! However, when the agent universalizes her maxim, she realizes that if everybody had always tried and would always try to act on this

---

[16] Herman (1993, pp. 73–93) offers further discussion on how we know when a maxim needs to be tested in the first place, citing so-called rules of moral salience.

[17] This is not to say that Kant has no account of value whatsoever: see in particular Section 5 on the end of humanity and Section 9 on Kant's notion of the highest good.

[18] Mill (1867, p. 5) and Hegel (1821/1991, p. 162) both make this mistake, but the misunderstanding appears as early as Hermann Andreas Pistorius's (1786) review of the *Groundwork*.

maxim, promises – whether they are false or not – would rarely if ever be believed. In order for her plan to work, she needs her friend to believe her when she says that she will pay back the loan. In universalizing the maxim, she thereby sees that she would undermine her own plan of action; it would be impossible to act on her individual maxim if that maxim were universalized.

Again, Kant's argument does not rest on the assertion that it would be bad or inconvenient if nobody believed promises. This might very well be the case: given the choice, we might well prefer to live in a world where promises are possible. But that would be a consequentialist argument that relied on a claim about the value of promise-keeping, presumably as a means toward happiness. Nor, it seems to me, is Kant's claim that there is a *purely* logical contradiction between the agent's own maxim and the universalized version of the maxim. This is evidenced by the fact that the agent can quite coherently consider both simultaneously as she tests her maxim! The contradiction only arises at the level of *action*. There is, in other words, a *practical* contradiction between the individual maxim and the universalized version of the maxim, since the agent could not possibly *act* on the original maxim under the universalized condition, in the sense that the means proposed in her maxim will no longer successfully bring about the end.[19]

Another, perhaps more commonsensical, way of putting the same point is to say that in cases in which the agent has an impermissible maxim, the maxim only works as a successful plan of action if she is the only one – or one of only a handful of people – who acts on that maxim.[20] Imagine this time that our agent wants to take her toddler to a movie and, knowing her child's temperament, suspects that the child will at some point become restless during the film. She has the choice of either going to the children's matinee or going to a regular showing. Not wishing to be disturbed by scores of *other* restless children, she decides on the regular showing, with a maxim along the lines of: "*In order to have a pleasant viewing experience, I will take my child to the regular showing, even though I suspect she will at some point be restless*." Notice that it is the making of an exception for herself that generates the problematic aspect of the maxim. Having the maxim to take one's restless toddler to the children's matinee is not at all problematic: that is the point of children's matinees! The problem arises when the agent wants to take advantage of the quiet atmosphere of the regular matinee – a quiet atmosphere she will probably disturb. There is

---

[19] But these points are somewhat controversial. See Korsgaard (1996, chapter 3) for more discussion of what type of contradiction is generated by impermissible maxims.

[20] This is true, at least, when it comes to what Kant will call "strict" or "perfect" duty. So-called imperfect duty is introduced in Section 4.3.

thus a sense in which Kant's universalization test captures those actions in which an agent seeks to make an exception for herself.

One might wonder at this stage whether Kant is simply presenting a sophisticated version of the golden rule as his moral theory. This is a reasonable suspicion, and some surface-level similarity between the two principles is not altogether surprising, since Kant takes his moral theory to reflect commonsensical notions of morality, some of which – like reciprocity – are represented in the golden rule. But, as Kant himself points out, there are some important differences between the two principles (*GMS*, 4:430n). Let us consider – as Kant himself does – the negative statement of the golden rule, that is, that one should not treat others as one would not wish to be treated. Stated this way, the golden rule might even be interpreted as a test of permissibility, just like the categorical imperative. The difference, however, is that the categorical imperative does not make permissibility contingent upon what an agent would wish for in her own case, but rather upon whether her maxim can be universalized. Second, the golden rule concerns itself only with how we ought to treat others but cannot provide an account of moral obligations that agents might have toward themselves. As we will see in what follows, Kant thinks that duties to the self are an important category of obligation. Finally, the golden rule provides a framework to determine which types of actions are prohibited, but it does not offer an account of duties of charity, for example. Of course, a positive formulation of the golden rule according to which we should "treat others as we would want to be treated" might offer more guidance on this last question, but it would still make these obligations contingent on the agent's specific ends or desires. As we will see in what follows, the categorical imperative accounts for duties of charity by appealing to a different sort of contradiction, not simply by asking what we would want.

## 4.2 Universal Law and Duties to the Self

An important feature of the formula of universal law is that it applies just as well to self-regarding maxims as it does to maxims that concern or involve other agents. Take the following example suggested by Onora O'Neill: Suppose I find it difficult, tedious, and at times downright depressing to follow the news carefully and make up my own mind about various political debates going on around me. I am inclined, as a result, just to let someone else tell me what I ought to think, whom I ought to support politically, and so on.[21] The maxim I formulate as a result is something like: "*In order to avoid the trouble of doing it myself, I will let others tell me what my opinions ought to be.*" Note that the

---

[21] O'Neill, 1975.

maxim straightforwardly generates the type of contradiction discussed above when universalized: if everyone were to attempt to act on the maxim, it would fail as a maxim, since in order to parrot someone else's political opinions, at least one other person has to have his or her own political opinions. Not surprisingly, the imperative to think for oneself emerges repeatedly as a moral, political, and epistemic virtue in Kant's writing.[22]

The elegance of O'Neill's example notwithstanding, it is worth noting that Kant's preferred example with respect to perfect duties to the self in the *Groundwork* is that of suicide. Kant imagines an agent "who feels weary of life because of a series of ills that has grown to the point of hopelessness" (*GMS*, 4:421) and who wishes to end his own suffering. The agent's maxim, as Kant describes it, is "from self-love I make it my principle to shorten my life if, when protracted any longer, it threatens more ill than it promises agreeableness" (GMS, 4:422). (We will have to set aside at this stage whether this aptly describes the maxim of a suicidal agent or to what extent some decisions to end one's life follow a maxim at all.) Kant argues that there is a sort of contradiction in the agent's universalized maxim, but his argument is perhaps not as seamless as one might hope: he observes that "a nature whose law it were to destroy life by means of the same sensation the function of which it is to impel toward the advancement of life, would contradict itself and would not thus subsist as a nature" (*GMS*, 4:422). In this particular example, at least, a contradiction is only generated if one assumes a teleological principle implicit in our tendencies toward self-preservation and self-fulfillment. But it is far from obvious that Kant can or should help himself to such a principle in the course of his argument. Kant's appeal to the example of suicide as a violation of a duty to oneself is, for these reasons, probably not his best argument regarding the existence or nature of duties to the self.[23] But other Kantian texts are rich with better, more compelling examples. The duty to think for oneself, as already noted, emerges as a central Kantian tenet in several other texts. Other important duties to oneself include a duty to avoid self-deception and a duty of self-respect.

## 4.3 Imperfect Duty and Demandingness

Thus far, we have only discussed one way that universalizing an impermissible maxim can generate a contradiction, namely, by bringing about a so-called

---

[22] For example, in Kant's famous essay "What is Enlightenment?"

[23] This interpretation follows Paton, 1971. One might alternatively argue that Kant is making a point about universalizing the suicidal maxim *across time*: there is perhaps a contradiction in suddenly using a "sensation" that has *up until this point* served to advance life to destroy it (see Glasgow, 2003). See also Uleman (2016) for a defense of the argument on foundational grounds.

*contradiction in conception*, according to which the agent's universalized maxim makes her initial plan of action impossible. It is impossible to even conceive of acting on the maxim when it is universalized because universalizing the maxim renders it impossible to act upon, that is, by robbing the proposed means of their ability to accomplish the end. When a universalized maxim generates a contradiction in conception, this indicates that the proposed course of action violates so-called perfect duty. We have, in other words, a strict duty to avoid acting on such a maxim.

Importantly, however, the categorical imperative procedure also identifies a second type of contradiction. This second type of contradiction, a *contradiction in willing*, corresponds to a different type of duty or obligation, so-called imperfect duty. To see how Kant's argument works, let us again begin with an example of a proposed maxim. Kant asks us to imagine an agent who doesn't wrong anyone, but who simply prefers not to help others (*GMS*, 4:423). His maxim is thus something like the following: "*When another person needs my help and I could help him, I will refrain from helping in order to preserve my own resources or pursue my own ends.*" What happens when we universalize this maxim? The maxim does not run afoul of the contradiction in the conception test: the agent could very easily act on this maxim, even in a world in which everyone else acted on the same maxim. What is more, Kant observes, that imagined world would probably be better than one in which everyone pays lip service to kindness and generosity but then tries to get away with cheating whenever they can. He certainly wouldn't be wronging anybody. What is the contradiction, then, if we can easily conceive of the agent acting on his maxim, even when it is universalized? Here, Kant argues, a contradiction exists between the universalized maxim and the agent's *own will*. Kant observes that each one of us is a finite being who necessarily needs the help of others from time to time, but to universalize the maxim of not helping would mean that we would never receive any assistance. We thus generate a contradiction between the *universalized maxim* ("nobody will ever help anybody") and our *own will* (the wish or need to be helped from time to time). It does not suffice to resolve the contradiction simply to announce that one will never wish for the help of others, in the way that a person might opt out of an insurance plan; this would be to deny the fact that we are fundamentally needy and dependent creatures. The German word that Kant uses in this context to describe the type of need we experience is *Noth* – indicating serious need or emergency, and not simply something we might like but could just as easily do without. There is thus a sense in which the person who refuses to help others makes two related mistakes: she makes an exception for herself by expecting help but never being willing to offer it, and she denies her nature as a finite, needy being.

When an agent's maxim generates a contradiction in willing when universalized, this indicates that the agent's maxim is impermissible. And since the impermissible maxim in this case is a maxim *not* to help, the result is that we have a duty to have a maxim to help others. Maxims that generate contradictions in willing thus generate positive duties (i.e. duties of commission). However, unlike the perfect duties generated by contradictions in conception, these positive duties are open-ended in the sense that there is typically more than one way to fulfill them. How, precisely, they are enacted can be contingent, for example, on the type of help that is needed and the agent's abilities at any given time.

The contradiction in willing generated by universalizing the maxim of non-beneficence tells us that we should *not* have a maxim of *never* helping others. But there is some debate among scholars regarding what an agent's maxim ought to be – how much she ought to help, or how often she ought to perform imperfect duty at the exclusion of other things she might do, particularly things she might like to do for the sake of her own pleasure or happiness. One thing is clear from what we have seen so far: the answer to this question will not depend on an account of a value (e.g. happiness or well-being) that ought to be maximized. For the utilitarian, this is in theory an easy answer – one ought to perform those actions that bring about the most happiness overall. On the utilitarian account, an agent who intentionally chooses an action out of self-interest at the expense of an other-regarding action that would bring about more happiness falls short morally. To spend money on a pair of shoes I don't need when I could put that money to better use donating it to Doctors Without Borders is a kind of moral *failure*. Now, of course, it is often difficult to know or predict what will actually bring about the most happiness, but in principle, at least, there is a clear consequentialist answer to the question of how much one ought to do: one ought to aim to maximize happiness, nothing less. Another way of putting this point is to say that for the consequentialist, there is a single scale of goodness, and one ought to always aim to do as much as one can to bring about as much goodness as possible.

However, as we have already seen, Kantian morality asks a question about *permissibility*, not maximization. And there are two ways that maxims can turn out to generate a contradiction and thus be impermissible. First, a maxim that includes some plan of action (e.g. theft, deception) can generate a contradiction in conception. In this case, the agent has a negative duty, or a duty of omission, to avoid acting on this maxim. If she nevertheless chooses to act on the maxim, then this will be a case of moral failure or viciousness. Kant sometimes denotes this kind of moral failure as a negative magnitude (e.g. $-a$ or $-1$). As we have just seen, a maxim that includes *inaction* can also fail – for example, the maxim never to help others. So, again, if an agent persists with this type of maxim despite its impermissibility as a matter of principle (as opposed to mere forgetfulness or weakness, for example), then having that maxim would also be a case of moral failure ($-a$ or $-1$). Of course, there is some epistemic difference when it comes to these two types of moral failure. In the first case, the theft or deceit is proof that the agent is acting on an impermissible maxim, whereas in the case of the maxim of non-beneficence, the instance of failure may not be as recognizable. Even in the latter case, however, there may be fairly reliable indicators. If, for example, a person could easily perform an action that would be of great assistance (imagine cases of easy rescue, for example) and still chooses not to, this will be a good indication that her underlying maxim is one of non-beneficence.[24]

Notice, however, that this picture is still incomplete. In particular, one might like to know not just what is required to avoid moral *failure* but, indeed, how much is required of us when it comes to the performance of charitable actions, for example. Because the Kantian decision procedure is a test of permissibility and not maximization, the question of what constitutes moral failure is separate from the question of what positive maxims (e.g. regarding charity) we ought to have. Let us consider two hypothetical agents to see this point. Both agents recognize that a duty of non-beneficence is impermissible, and so both adopt some form of helping maxim. The first agent recognizes her duties of beneficence and has a donation to Oxfam taken out of her bank account every month. Perhaps she also volunteers time or money when opportunities arise in her community, but when the accounting is done, she spends *more* money and time on her own interests and hobbies. A second agent devotes much more time and money – perhaps close to all of her spare time and money – to charitable causes. Kant would describe the maxims of both agents as virtuous, sometimes denoting this using positive magnitudes ($+a$ or $+1$). Still, it seems one agent is more committed to helping others than the other. Is there a sense in which the second agent is morally better than the first? Should we all aim to be more like the second agent?

Kant's answer, I think, is that the second agent is more virtuous than the first and that we should aim to have an attitude toward helping others that is more like the second person's attitude, but that the first agent still has a perfectly acceptable (i.e. non-vicious) maxim. This is because, in Kant's view, an agent is more virtuous the closer her maxim comes to an ideal. That ideal, insofar as Kant ever comes close to stating it, is for an agent to "bring wide obligation

---

[24] See Baron, 1995 and Stohr, 2011. See Sticker, 2019 for an in-depth discussion of cases of easy rescue.

[imperfect duty] as close as possible to the concept of narrow obligation [perfect duty]" (*DV*, 6:391). Crucially, however, this is not an imperative to maximize an outcome, nor is it an indictment of the first agent. Since Kantian ethics is concerned with maxims rather than actions or outcomes, it is ill-suited to measuring a person's virtue by how much of one's salary one donates to charity or how many luxuries one sacrifices. Rather, it involves an injunction to have a particular sort of maxim – one that takes what we might call an attitude of strictness toward imperfect duty. There is thus a sense in which Kantian ethics is demanding, since an agent can almost always be more virtuous in some way or another. On the other hand, failure to be as virtuous as possible is not the same as viciousness, and striving for the kind of virtue described here is an ongoing, lifelong goal.[25]

## 4.4 Some Criticisms of the Formula of Universal Law

It is worth pausing briefly to consider some objections to the formula of universal law, as presented thus far. Perhaps the most common of these is the worry that the categorical imperative procedure generates so-called false negatives and false positives, that is, that applying the categorical imperative procedure to certain maxims will result in some perfectly innocuous maxims being deemed impermissible and some patently impermissible or vicious maxims being deemed permissible. As an example of the former, consider the example of playing tennis on Sunday morning when most other people are in church, in order to be guaranteed a court.[26] The agent's maxim, in this case, is something like, "*In order to guarantee myself a court, I will play tennis on Sunday morning when my neighbors are in church.*" The maxim seems innocent enough, but notice that when the maxim is universalized, it appears to undermine itself and generate a contradiction in conception. If *everyone* had and acted on this maxim, the tennis courts would no longer be empty on Sunday mornings. A similar problem appears to arise when it comes to maxims that seem obviously impermissible, too. Consider the maxim: "*In order to get some quick money, I will rob a bank on the corner of Main Street and 4th Avenue at 3:22 p.m. on a sunny day during a leap year.*" Setting aside the legal trouble our agent would certainly find himself in if he were to be apprehended, it might seem as though the maxim would turn out to be permissible, since universalizing such

---

[25] It bears noting that there is debate about the question of "demandingness" in Kant's ethics and that this interpretation tends toward the more demanding interpretation. Other interpretations and arguments to consider include Baron, 1995; Formosa and Sticker, 2019; Hill, 1992; and Timmermann, 2018a.

[26] The example is borrowed from Herman, 1993.

a specific maxim would still leave the institutions and practices of banks in place.

However, in response to these worries, it will be important to ask what, precisely, the agent's maxim is. Is it her maxim to play tennis only when her neighbors are in church, or to rob banks only in very specific places and at very specific times? Most likely, it is not. Agents who aren't trying to manipulate their maxims so that they pass a universalization test have maxims to play tennis when the courts are not too busy (in the innocent case) and rob banks when in need of money (in the vicious case). To illustrate the point, consider a person who wants to return to the city from a beach vacation without getting stuck in traffic. She might consider the maxim "in order to avoid getting stuck in traffic, I will skip the afternoon at the beach and depart for the city right after breakfast." On its face, this seems an entirely prudent and morally unproblematic maxim. What would the categorical imperative have to say about this maxim? One obvious worry arises, namely, that if everyone acted on the same maxim (to leave early in order to beat traffic), the maxim would clearly be unable to accomplish its stated end. (Indeed, things would be even worse, from the standpoint of the agent, since she would have sacrificed a day at the beach only to sit in traffic!) But on closer inspection, it seems that the precise time of day at which the agent departs is not essential to the maxim. What is essential to the maxim is the agent's decision to leave the beach earlier (or later) than most other drivers. Now, of course, others might have that more general maxim as well, and this might result in the shifting of popular departure times. But this is a coordination problem, not a contradiction. And in practice, even a coordination problem is unlikely, since leaving early means sacrificing a day at the beach and leaving late means arriving home very late in the evening. In other words, in this example, there are incentives that argue in favor of the decision to leave the beach in the late afternoon (i.e. the desire to enjoy one last day at the beach but not to arrive at home too late). The person who chooses to leave the beach early (or late) opts to forgo one of these ends.

Now, consider another person similarly disinclined to sit in traffic on the way home from vacation. However, this agent is also disinclined to miss her last day at the beach or to arrive home late in the evening. She also knows that there is an emergency travel lane running parallel to the highway and that there are rarely police patrolling the highway on such busy travel days. She formulates the maxim: "*In order to avoid getting stuck in traffic, I will drive in the emergency lane in order to bypass the row of cars.*" Notice that there is a sense in which this maxim clearly only works if the agent is able to make an exception for herself. If everyone were to have the same maxim, the maxim would clearly not be able to accomplish its end. Now, one might object that there is only an apparent difference between the two cases, perhaps because one maxim includes the agent's doing something illegal, which the other does not. And it is relevant to the example that driving in the emergency lane is (usually) illegal, since this is what prevents most people from doing it. But the maxim is not impermissible simply because it is outlawed. What makes the maxim problematic is that the agent exempts herself from a practice in order to take advantage of everyone else's compliance with it. This is notably *not* the case with the early-leaving example. In this sense, the maxim to drive in the emergency lane shares this important feature with, for example, the false promising example. That maxim also relies on the agent's excepting himself from some coordinated activity, as, we might add, does the maxim to rob a bank. Indeed, any attempt to describe the bank-robbing maxim in artificially narrow terms is likely an attempt to rationalize its permissibility ex post facto.

## 4.5 The Categorical Imperative and Moral Skepticism

Of course, there is another worry regarding the formula of universal law: we might call this the skeptical worry, expressed by the person who just doesn't care that her maxim is not universalizable and only works if she makes an exception for herself. Surely, she will point out, *inconsistency* itself is not immoral! There is a sense in which this is correct but also a sense in which it misses an important point about Kant's argument. It is crucial to remember that Kant's aim in describing the formula of universal law is not to prove that morality exists (i.e. that we are bound by it), but rather to show that *if* we are in fact bound by some moral code, then that moral code must be the categorical imperative. The skeptic who is unmoved by the contradiction implicit in her universalized maxim may not be disagreeing with Kant that there is a contradiction when the maxim is universalized. Her disagreement with Kant most likely rests on one of two points: First, she may think that morality exists (i.e. that we do have some moral obligations), but that Kant's principle fails to accurately describe the content of those obligations. Second, she may be a skeptic about morality in general, that is, she thinks that morality is a fiction. Kant has a reply to both worries.

To the first worry – that morality exists, but that he has incorrectly identified its principle – Kant would surely wonder what other principle of morality there could possibly be. Recall that Kant takes his account of the principle of morality to be the only possible account that accommodates the necessity and universality of a moral law (*GMS*, 4:443). All other principles run afoul of this criterion. All forms of consequentialism assume or argue for some value to be effected or maximized, but all of these ends are contingent; as far as Kant is concerned, none carries with it the absolute necessity required for law. Various forms of moral sense theory have a moral principle that is dependent upon the affective responses of an actual, or sometimes ideal, agent. But these, too, are contingent. Moral principles based on custom or indoctrination fare poorly on this score as well, since these are entirely contingent upon whatever custom dictates. Insofar as one agrees with Kant that the moral law must be necessary and universal, he thinks that the categorical imperative is the only live candidate.

What about the second version of the skeptical worry, namely, the amoralist's objection that morality is a fiction? Kant does not have an answer, as such, to this skeptical worry. Indeed, there is an important sense in which he simply *cannot* have an answer to this skeptical worry without undermining his entire theory. This is because any extra-moral consideration that Kant could appeal to would undermine the standards of necessity and universality that, on his view, lie at the foundation of any account of the moral law. Imagine, for example, if Kant were to try to convince the amoralist by arguing that following the categorical imperative is the strategy most likely to bring about one's own well-being. This strategy might give the skeptic a reason to accept the categorical imperative as a guiding principle, but it would come at the cost of necessity and universality, since bringing about well-being (and all of its attendant contingencies) would then serve as the ultimate foundation of morality.[27] But this is not to say that Kant has no response whatsoever to the skeptic. Although he cannot appeal to external reasons or values to show us that we ought to be committed to morality, he does sometimes offer arguments to show that we are already implicitly committed to morality or that we already endorse morality. We can begin to see the shape of Kant's argument when we consider his notion of humanity (Section 5), and further argument along these lines emerges in his discussion of autonomy and freedom (Sections 7 and 8).

## 5 The Moral Law: The Formula of Humanity

Thus far in the discussion, we have been emphasizing the important fact that Kant's ethics is a non-teleological theory – this is to say that it does not begin with or depend upon an account of an end or value that ought to be pursued or maximized. But it is important to note that Kant's theory is not devoid of ends altogether. Indeed, Kant acknowledges that all willing requires some end, and this will include moral willing. However, Kant thinks that action for the sake of a contingent, desired end is very different from action for the sake of a necessary, moral end. This section will explore the necessary end of moral

---

[27] The problem may bring to mind the dilemma described in Prichard, 1912.

action, something that Kant calls humanity. We also consider how action that takes humanity as its end differs from other end-directed action.

## 5.1 Hypothetical Imperatives and the Categorical Imperative

When we act for the sake of some desired end, we act on what Kant calls a hypothetical imperative. We have already discussed hypothetical imperatives (Section 3), albeit without explicitly labeling them as such. Recall that any action must have an objective determining ground – a principle or rule that we refer to in order to guide our action. When we act for the sake of inclination, this objective determining ground is a hypothetical imperative. It is an *imperative* because it tells us that we ought to do something, but it is *hypothetical* because it only applies to an agent hypothetically, that is, *if* she has a particular end or has settled upon some goal. A hypothetical imperative is informed by empirical facts and causal laws in order to tell us how to achieve whatever end we set for ourselves on the basis of inclination. Imagine I have a meeting in the morning and want to make sure that I arrive at work on time. The operative hypothetical imperative in this case would take into account various facts about the world (that I have a car, that I need to drop children off at school, that traffic is heavy, etc.) and tell me that if I want to arrive at work on time, I will need to leave the house at least an hour beforehand and take a certain route. Importantly, if I cease to have the relevant end (perhaps I decide I can skip the meeting or attend the meeting remotely), then the hypothetical imperative no longer applies to me. After all, it would be very odd for me to pursue means toward an end that I no longer have – for example, if I drove all the way to work, having already decided to attend the meeting from home. On the other hand, if I do adopt some end, then, in Kant's view, I also adopt the necessary means toward that end. In other words, as soon as I decide to pursue an end, the relevant hypothetical imperatives apply to me. My adoption of an end is precisely what makes the hypothetical imperative *an imperative for me.*

Though there are at least as many hypothetical imperatives as there are ends, Kant thinks that there are two general types of hypothetical imperative.[28] Imperatives of skill apply when an agent adopts some particular end that others may or may not share. The examples we've seen so far – dressmaking and getting to work on time – involve imperatives of skill, since not everyone shares the end of making a dress or getting to work on time. Imperatives of prudence,

---

[28] Here, I assume that there are multiple hypothetical imperatives, each corresponding to the end it seeks to accomplish. But there is some debate in the literature about Kant's classification of hypothetical imperatives, in particular, whether there is just one hypothetical imperative or whether there are several. See in particular Hill, 1973; Kohl, 2018; Papish, 2018; Schroeder, 2005; Timmermann, 2007; and Wood, 2013.

on the other hand, are hypothetical imperatives that aim at an end that Kant thinks all agents do, in fact, share as a result of their sensible nature, namely, the end of happiness. But although all agents share the general end of happiness, how to achieve this end is indeterminate and contingent for a multitude of reasons. First, there is the obvious point that different things will make different people happy, even if some things (e.g. health, wealth, friendship) are generally conducive to happiness. But even setting that point aside, we can often be mistaken about what will make us happy in the future or misjudge the relative strength of our various constituent ends. And even when we correctly predict what sorts of things will bring us happiness, conditions can change, such that the things that once brought us happiness no longer do. The contingency associated with the pursuit of happiness is part of the reason that Kant thinks that happiness could never serve as the foundation of morality, even though he acknowledges that it is an end that all agents do, in fact, share.

Now, as we have seen, when we act for the sake of morality, our wills refer to a different objective determining ground in order to guide our action – this is the categorical imperative. As an imperative, it is action-guiding, but as a *categorical* imperative, it does not apply to us hypothetically, or only if we have certain ends. Instead, it applies to us categorically, that is, necessarily and no matter what our particular ends might be. Crucially, however, the categorical imperative also has an end. However, this is not an end that some people *might* have or an end, however indeterminate, that all people *do*, in fact, have. Rather, the end associated with the categorical imperative is an end that all agents *must* have, or ought to have.

Although hypothetical imperatives and the categorical imperative are both objective determining grounds of the will, it is crucial to note some differences between them, since to think of them as parallel or strictly analogous can often lead to misunderstandings about one or the other. First, hypothetical imperatives begin with and are made practical by the end that the agent adopts on the basis of desire.[29] In other words, a hypothetical imperative, all by itself, doesn't give the agent a motive to act. Rather, it is the end that the agent sets or adopts that provides this reason. A hypothetical imperative is a bit like an instruction manual: it tells an agent how to accomplish an end or satisfy a desire that she might have, just as an instruction manual might tell a person how to put together a piece of furniture. But if a person has no intention of building a piece of furniture, the instruction manual that she finds lying in a drawer is just a booklet of instructions – it doesn't give her a reason to do anything. To make a more

---

[29] This is at least the impression one typically gets from reading Kant's texts. Strictly speaking, however, moral ends could also generate hypothetical imperatives, for example, *"If I want to help my friend through a difficult time, I should ask what I can do for her."*

physical analogy, the hypothetical imperative is a bit like the gear on a bicycle – it translates a desire or end into action or movement. But the gear isn't what moves a bicycle; the person pushing on the pedals moves the bicycle. Similarly, the principle expressed by the hypothetical imperative is inert without the desire or end.

It is thus difficult to overstate the importance of the ends that agents set on the basis of desire when it comes to hypothetical imperatives. If an agent adopts an end, then she adopts the means toward that end. But we might wonder: What about cases in which a person seems to adopt an end but then fails to adopt the relevant means? Surely it is all too common for us to have the end of arriving at work on time but then also decide to squeeze in one more email or cup of coffee before we leave the house. Does this mean we are weak-willed? Irrational? Both? Kant's answer seems to be that weakness of will – that is, adopting the end but not having the strength of will to carry through the relevant action – is, practically speaking, impossible. Adopting an end is just to put a particular hypothetical imperative into action; if I adopt an end, I necessarily adopt the means toward that end (*GMS*, 4:417). Conversely, if I cease to pursue the means toward an end, I no longer pursue the end. If I know that I need to leave the house an hour before my meeting and I nevertheless pour myself another cup of coffee when I should be leaving, then I have abandoned my original end, at least temporarily. Of course, I might also be engaging in some degree of rationalizing or wishful thinking, such that my principle of action becomes faulty. I might (incorrectly) say to myself, "*Well, it is Friday, and traffic is usually a bit lighter on Fridays, so I probably have an extra ten minutes today.*" When it comes to hypothetical imperatives, it does seem as though this type of irrationality is possible in Kant's view, even if the weakness of will is, strictly speaking, not.

What about the end associated with the categorical imperative? Although the categorical imperative also has an end (more on this in a moment), it does not apply – like the booklet of furniture instructions – only if you adopt that end. The categorical imperative, if we can excuse taking the metaphor in a somewhat absurd direction, would be like a booklet of furniture instructions that tells you that you *must necessarily*, in no uncertain terms, build a bookcase, no matter how many books you may or may not have and no matter what else you happen to have planned. Hypothetical and categorical imperatives are both imperatives, but as this example demonstrates, they are completely different with respect to the way they command and with respect to the source of their imperatival force.

Note, too, that the end demanded by the categorical imperative will be an altogether different sort of end from the ends associated with the hypothetical imperative. The end required by the categorical imperative does not become an end only if an agent chooses to endorse or pursue it; it is a necessary end brought to light, as it were, by the categorical imperative. It is, as Kant will often say, "an end in itself." This also means that the end associated with the categorical imperative will require a different type of action for its sake. Actions that aim at the ends of hypothetical imperatives pursue, promote, and sometimes maximize these ends; their aim is to *bring about* these contingent ends. In the case of the necessary end of the categorical imperative, the idea is not to bring about the end in question, still less bring about as much of the end as possible. Rather, actions that "aim" at this end will be ones that serve to protect this end or to help it flourish. But what, exactly, is the necessary end of the categorical imperative? That is the question we turn to next.

## 5.2 Humanity as an End in Itself

Identifying and proving the existence (or reality) of the necessary end of the categorical imperative is no small matter. Indeed, if Kant can show that there is such a necessary end, he will have also demonstrated the so-called validity of the moral law. Recall that much of Kant's argument in the first two sections of the *Groundwork* is provisional – he intends only to show that *if* there is a moral law that binds or obligates us necessarily and universally, then it would have to be the categorical imperative. However, the merely provisional nature of Kant's argument changes when the possibility of a necessary end comes onto the scene. This is because if Kant can show that a necessary end does, in fact, exist, then he will have simultaneously shown that there is something that necessarily obligates us to act in accordance with the categorical imperative. To prove the reality of this necessary end just is to argue that we are bound by the moral law whose end it is. Kant thus muses: "But suppose there were something *the existence of which in itself* has an absolute worth, that, as an *end in itself*, could be a ground of determinate laws, then the ground of a possible categorical imperative, *i.e.* of a practical law, would lie in it, and only in it alone" (*GMS*, 4:428).

Immediately after wondering about the possibility of the necessary end of the categorical imperative, Kant rather boldly asserts: "Now I say: a human being and generally every rational being *exists* as an end in itself, *not merely as a means* for the discretionary use for this or that will, but must in all its actions, whether directed towards itself or also to other rational beings, always be considered *at the same time as an end*" (*GMS*, 4:428). With this sentence, Kant introduces humanity, the necessary end at which the moral law aims and which gives the moral law its validity.[30] When a person acts on the objective

---

[30] The discussion that follows describes humanity as a capacity. Note, however, that there is debate about whether "rational nature," another term Kant sometimes uses, refers to a capacity or whether it refers to rational *beings*, as perhaps suggested at *GMS*, 4:428.

determining ground of the categorical imperative, she thus acts for the sake of respecting or preserving humanity or helping humanity flourish, whether in her own person or in the person of another.

But what, precisely, is humanity? It is clear from the passages cited previously, along with many others, that humanity has something to do with a rational nature found in human beings. Despite the term, being a member of the species *homo sapiens* is by no means necessary for humanity – nothing in Kant's account stands in the way of someday discovering that other creatures have the capacity of humanity, for example. But what sort of rationality does the capacity for humanity describe? It is clear that humanity has to do with practical rationality – that is, reasoning about action and acting on the basis of such reasoning. In some passages, Kant suggests that humanity is the capacity to set and pursue ends, that is, the capacity to set an end and act according to a hypothetical imperative in pursuit of that end. So, for example, he notes that, "A rational nature is distinguished from the others by this, that it sets itself an end" (*GMS*, 4:437). And in another text, he defines humanity as the capacity to "set oneself an end at all" (*DV*, 6:392).[31] In other passages, however, Kant appears to describe humanity more narrowly, as a strictly moral capacity – for example, when he claims that "morality is the condition under which alone a rational being can be an end in itself" (*GMS*, 4:435). As we discuss the formula of humanity and Kant's arguments (or potential arguments) for humanity's being a necessary end, we will discuss these two competing definitions in more detail. For the time being, however, it is worth noting that the capacity to set and pursue ends and the capacity for morality, though different in ways that we have discussed already, do share the quality of being forms of willing, that is, of acting under the representation of a law. What is more, in practical terms, the two definitions of humanity tend to pick out the same individuals as deserving of respect according to the moral law. That is, although there could in theory be agents capable of acting on hypothetical imperatives but not categorical imperatives, Kant seems clearly to think that the two capacities come as a pair, even in individuals who do not live up to the demands of morality. Take, for example, Kant's discussion of the "hardened scoundrel" in the *Groundwork*. Kant argues that:

> [T]here is no one, not even the most hardened scoundrel, if only he is
> otherwise in the habit of using reason, who – when one presents him with
> examples of probity of purpose, of steadfastness in following good maxims,
> of compassion and of general benevolence (involving in addition great

---

[31] Following an updated translation of the *Doctrine of Virtue* by Jeanine Grenberg and Jens Timmermann (Cambridge University Press, forthcoming).

sacrifices of advantages and comfort) – does not wish that he too might be so disposed (*GMS*, 4:454).

But what is Kant's argument for the claim that humanity exists as a necessary end or as an end in itself? It is important to note that when Kant introduces humanity in the second section of the *Groundwork* and then immediately announces ("now I say … ") that it is the necessary end of moral willing, he is not yet attempting to provide an *argument* for the claim that humanity is an end in itself. Indeed, in a footnote, he reassures the reader that at this stage, the claim is merely a postulate, and he promises to provide an argument for it in the final section of the book, and even there, it is not obvious where the argument is to be found. Still, this remark itself gives us some important insight into the argument that Kant will ultimately attempt to provide, since the final section of the book aims to show that rational agents are bound by the moral law because they have a certain type of will, specifically, the one that is not in every case determined by external forces and is capable of its own spontaneous determination. Kant's argument for the claim that humanity is an end in itself will thus have something to do with the argument that our wills are free and that we are bound by the moral law.[32] We will return to this puzzle in Section 8.

It should be emphasized that the task of arguing for the absolute worth of humanity is as difficult as it is important to Kant's project. Establishing humanity's status as an end in itself is in a sense the "million dollar question" in Kant's moral philosophy – to prove this is to demonstrate the validity or bindingness of the categorical imperative. There is thus unsurprisingly a large literature offering interpretations of Kant's argument or arguments in support of Kant's claim.[33] Though this discussion cannot provide a survey of these, one of the most famous and influential arguments in this vein is offered by Christine Korsgaard.[34] Korsgaard argues that our rational capacity to set and pursue ends is a capacity, as it were, to confer value on particular ends. But, Korsgaard argues, this value-conferring capacity must have its own, intrinsic value or worth. Korsgaard's argument has inspired a good deal of commentary in its own right. Note, too, that the argument seems to work best if we conceive of humanity as the capacity to set and pursue ends. If, however, one adopts the view that humanity is limited to the narrower capacity to act according to moral principles, then Korsgaard's argument may capture a definition of rationality that is too broad. One can begin to see how difficult these questions become for readers and interpreters of Kant.

---

[32] Cf. Guyer, 1998.

[33] For example, Dean, 2006; Guyer, 1998; Martin, 2006; Timmermann, 2006.

[34] Korsgaard, 1996.

## 5.3 The Formula of Humanity

For now, let us set to one side the arguments for the absolute worth of humanity and return to Kant's exposition of the concept and its role in formulating a universal and necessary moral principle. As the necessary end of action guided by the categorical imperative, humanity yields its own formulation of the categorical imperative, which Kant states as follows: "*So act that you use humanity, in your own person as well as in the person of any other, always at the same time as an end, never merely as a means*" (*GMS*, 4:429). Notice that the formula of humanity, in its most straightforward statement, simply requires that we treat humanity, wherever we find it, as an end that has absolute worth, that is, as an end that cannot be compared to or traded for some contingent end. However, the imperative to treat humanity always as an end in itself contains two parts, as it were. First, there is a negative duty never to treat humanity (in one's own person or in that of another) as merely a means to an end. This means that one ought never to act on a maxim that requires one to treat humanity as a mere tool or that destroys or otherwise harms humanity for the sake of some contingent end. Second, even in cases in which one successfully avoids violating this negative duty, there is still a duty to help humanity flourish. These two parts correspond, as we will see in what follows, to perfect and imperfect duty. Let us consider how this formulation of the imperative responds to the four examples discussed previously in Section 4.

(1) Suicide. There is a sense in which the formula of humanity has a much easier time responding to the person whose maxim it is to end one's life in order to stop unbearable suffering or unhappiness. After all, to end one's life is also to destroy one's own humanity. But, Kant points out, this would be to destroy something with absolute worth for the sake of something (i.e. happiness or well-being) that only has contingent value. To follow through on this particular maxim would be to dispose of one's humanity for the sake of happiness.[35] Still, one might reasonably wonder about other maxims of self-destruction, for example, the maxim to sacrifice one's life in order to save another person's life or to preserve one's dignity. Though Kant appears to insist that even these sorts of maxims are impermissible, we might wonder if the same reasoning applies, since it's not as obvious in such cases that the agent is destroying or throwing away her humanity for the sake of some contingent end like happiness.[36]

Earlier, we also considered how the maxim of not thinking for oneself might be impermissible according to the formula of universal law. We can see quite

---

[35] But see Langton, 1992 for a discussion that calls this interpretation of the maxim into question.

[36] Kant considers some examples like these in the context of "casuistical questions" in his later work, the *Metaphysics of Morals* (*MS*, 6:423–424).

easily why such a maxim would not be consistent with the formula of humanity, either. Though the agent in question does not destroy his humanity permanently or irrevocably, as in the case of the suicidal maxim, it is nevertheless the case that his is a maxim to take his rational capacity "off line" as it were, merely for the sake of pleasure or desire. For the same reason, Kant would certainly object to the maxim of getting drunk with the aim of dulling or numbing one's rational capacities for some time (*DV*, 6:427). Taking a nap or going under anesthesia for a medically necessary procedure do not pose the same moral risk, since these are done for the sake of health and self-preservation.

(2) False Promise. Recall that the agent's maxim in the case of false promising is to make a promise she has no intention of keeping in order to secure some money. Kant's gloss of what is wrong with this maxim according to the formula of humanity is worth quoting in full. He argues that,

> [S]omeone who has it in mind to make a lying promise to others will see at once that he wants to make use of another human being merely as a means, who does not at the same time contain in himself the end. For the one I want to use for my purposes by such a promise cannot possibly agree to my way of proceeding with him and thus himself contain the end of this action.
>
> (*GMS*, 4:429)

Note that in the case of false promising, we are not destroying humanity, as in the case of suicide. But one needn't destroy humanity in order to treat it as a mere means to one's end. In the case of the false promise, I treat another person as a mere means because I treat her as a tool to accomplish my goal. The point is particularly clear in the case of the false promise because in order for my maxim to succeed, I need the other agent to believe me when I promise to repay the loan and then choose to act on this false belief. There is thus a sense in which my false promise makes it impossible for her to make her own choice in the matter. Consider, for example, if I instead told her the truth: that I needed money but had no intention of repaying it. In that case, the other agent is able to make her own choice: perhaps she will just give me the money after all. What makes all the difference is that she is able to consider her options and make her own choice on the basis of the facts available to her. Of course, in the latter case, I am still using my friend as a means. But this is perfectly acceptable: agents use one another as means in unproblematic ways all the time. A moral problem arises only when one agent uses the other *merely* as a means to her end.

The inability to use one's own deliberative capacity and make one's own choice, as previously described, is what Kant describes as "not being able to contain the end of the action in himself" or as not being able to "agree" with the maxim (*GMS*, 4:430). Philosophers have sometimes described this state as one of not being able to consent to the other person's action, and this can be a useful way of thinking about the nature of the moral failure and the way in which these maxims fail to respect the absolute worth of humanity in another person.

(3) Developing Talents. The formula of humanity finds objection to laziness, or the failure to develop talents, not because this uses humanity as a mere means to an end but because the agent fails to foster or promote humanity in her own person. To neglect one's talents, Kant argues, "would perhaps be consistent with the *preservation* of humanity, as an end in itself, but not with the *advancement* of this end" (*GMS*, 4:430). Two important points stand out in the context of this argument. First, Kant seems implicitly to define humanity in the broader sense here, that is, as denoting a more general capacity to set and pursue one's ends, rather than just the narrower capacity for moral reasoning. If humanity were merely the capacity for moral reasoning, it would be difficult to see how the failure to develop one's talents would interfere with the advancement of humanity, particularly if the development of these talents did not otherwise contribute to moral ends. Second, we begin to get a clearer sense of what our duties with respect to humanity in oneself and others entail – our obligation is not just to protect humanity from destruction or manipulation but also to foster and promote it. This point comes across clearly in the argument for a duty of beneficence.

(4) Beneficence. As with laziness, non-beneficence does not violate humanity, in the sense that it does not use humanity as a mere means to an end. Kant admits that "humanity could indeed subsist if no one contributed anything to the happiness of others while not intentionally detracting anything from it" (*GMS*, 4:430). Failing to be beneficent in any particular case does not use another as a mere means; however, non-beneficence does fail to *promote* humanity – it would still only constitute a "negative and not positive agreement with *humanity, as an end in itself*" if everyone does not also try, as far as he can, to advance the ends of others" (*GMS*, 4:430). What does it mean to "advance the ends of others"? As we have already seen, the imperative admits of more and less "demanding" interpretations (see Section 4.3). Minimally, however, it means doing what one can to advance the ends and projects of others, and this can sometimes mean tending to the fundamental needs of others. Importantly, however, one should not impose ends or projects on others, since this sort of paternalism would itself violate the formula of humanity (*MS*, 6:454).

## 6 Respect for the Law and Action from Duty

Having explored several formulations of Kant's categorical imperative, along with how these relate to his account of willing, we are in a good position to consider briefly his account of moral motivation. The distinction between hypothetical imperatives and the categorical imperative that we have been exploring demonstrates that acting for the sake of morality will require its own, distinctive, type of motivation. When we act according to a hypothetical imperative, we act because we have an interest in the relevant end in the form of an inclination or desire. When we act for the sake of the categorical imperative, however, we do not act for the sake of inclination. Rather, Kant will argue, we are moved by respect for the law itself. Thus, he notes: "[A]ll moral *interest*, so-called, consists solely in *respect* for the law" (*GMS*, 4:401n).

In the *Groundwork of the Metaphysics of Morals*, the first inkling of a uniquely moral type of motivation is probably Kant's discussion of the various types of incentives we can have to act in a way that is consistent with what morality requires (*GMS*, 4:397–399). There, Kant makes a distinction among four different types of action as part of his examination of good willing and the concept of duty, intended to bring us closer to a statement of the supreme principle of morality, or the categorical imperative. The first type of action is action contrary to duty; Kant quickly sets this aside, since his strategy is to examine the various motives a person might have for acting in accord with duty. The second type of action is action that accords with morality, but which has self-interested motives. Here, we encounter Kant's famous example of the shopkeeper who charges even inexperienced customers a fair price because this is ultimately to his advantage – say, because having a reputation as a fair and upstanding merchant is good for business. Like the second type of action, the third type of action is one in which the agent acts in accord with duty out of inclination. However, unlike the second type of action, this inclination is not self-interested, but rather an immediate inclination to do as duty requires. Kant's examples include the immediate inclination to preserve our own lives and the immediate inclination to be beneficent that a "friend of humanity" has when he helps others. Finally, Kant points to the fourth type of action, the one in which the agent acts according to duty but not from inclination – that is, neither from self-interested inclination nor from immediate inclination. Here, Kant asks us to imagine, to take an example, a person who preserves his life despite great sorrow or a person who helps others despite its not bringing him any immediate joy. This type of agent acts from the motive of duty alone. Kant takes it to be a matter of common sense that there is something special about the fourth type of action. Only action from duty, in Kant's view, has moral worth.

There is some degree of irony, perhaps, in the fact that Kant took himself to be shining a light on a relatively commonsensical attitude toward duty and moral motivation, since he was almost immediately criticized for having an objectionable stance on moral motivation. In particular, it might seem as though Kant privileges motivation from duty when it runs counter to what inclination would have us do. But, surely, we think that the person who performs her duty gladly or cheerfully is in some sense more virtuous than the person who finds herself constantly overcoming inclination in order to act dutifully. The most memorable statement of this objection is probably Friedrich Schiller's poetic quip:[37]

> *Scruples of Conscience*
> Gladly I serve my friends, but alas I do it with inclination
> Hence I am frequently nagged by my lack of virtue.
> *Decision*
> There is no other advice, thou must seek to despise them,
> And do with disgust what thy duty commands.[38]

Schiller is certainly not alone in putting forward this type of objection; contemporary discussions of Kant's ethics sometimes raise the same sort of concern.[39] But in assessing the criticism, it is worth separating several components of it and examining each individually. The first worry may be that it seems counterintuitive to suggest that acting from duty must always be unpleasant or done reluctantly. Again, one might think that the person with an immediate inclination to be charitable is in some sense more virtuous than the person who acts only out of duty or who experiences a constant, nagging tension between inclination and morality. But Kant is by no means insisting that virtue or moral worth requires a struggle to overcome contravening inclination. The examples that Kant uses to demonstrate action from duty in the *Groundwork* are set up this way simply because our motives are obscure, even to ourselves. Kant has no way of identifying and highlighting the motive of duty other than to imagine examples where it is the *only possible motive* for the agent's action. And even if we think that there is something virtuous about overcoming inclinations when they get in the way of acting morally, there is no reason to think that overcoming more inclinations makes us more virtuous. Indeed, in Kant's view, the most virtuous person would probably be the person who strives to experience as little of this sort of interior struggle as possible.

Still, Schiller's criticism goes deeper than this – one might also wonder about Kant's claim that only action from duty has the special status of having moral worth, or deserving esteem. What could be more virtuous than a person whose immediate motive is to be beneficent, without a second thought for self-interest or advantage? Understanding Kant's answer to this objection helps make his

---

[37] Though as Wood (1999) observes, the poem is probably satirical. As Baxley (2010) points out, Schiller's more nuanced criticism of Kantian motivation appears in his *On Grace and Dignity*.

[38] The translation is from Timmermann, 2007.

[39] In particular, Stocker, 1976 and Williams, 1981. But see excellent responses by Baron, 1984, 2008; Guyer, 1993, chapter 10; and Herman, 1993, chapter 1.

precise position clear. As he sees it, there is very little difference between the immediate inclination to help and the inclination to help whose source is, for example, the love of honor. And this is because, as inclinations, both only contingently lead to action that is in accord with morality. As he puts it in the *Groundwork*:

> But I assert that in such a case an action of this kind – however much it conforms with duty, however amiable it may be – still has no true moral worth, but stands on the same footing as other inclinations, e.g. the inclination to honour, which if it fortunately lights upon what is in fact the general interest and in conformity with duty . . . deserves praise and encouragement, but not high esteem. (*GMS*, 4:398)

When an action in accord with duty is motivated by an immediate inclination, whether or not one has that immediate motivation is always a contingent matter – people are constituted differently, and even in a person who normally has beneficent inclinations, moods or states of affairs can shift this inclination. To put the point a different way: in order to know that a person has a good will, we need to know that the moral law determines their will directly and not via some contingent inclination.

It is also crucial at this stage to point out that despite initial appearances, Kant is not offering a rubric according to which we are to judge other people's maxims. The discussion of action from duty in the first section *Groundwork* has a very limited purpose, and this is to bring to the front of our minds one of three common sense "propositions" that helps bring the supreme principle of morality, the categorical imperative, to light. This commonsense proposition, as we have just seen, is that only action from the motive of duty leads non-contingently to moral action. In any case, motives (those of others and even our own) are obscure, so it is strictly speaking impossible to engage in an assessment of others' motives with the aim of gauging the moral worth of their maxims. Indeed, insofar as the discussion of motivation in the first section of the *Groundwork* offers any criteria according to which we can judge maxims, it is our *own* maxims that Kant thinks we should be interrogating. One type of moral error that Kant thinks we may be particularly susceptible to is a tendency toward over-congratulation or thinking of ourselves as effortlessly virtuous. Though our motives are also obscure to us, we can still benefit morally from asking ourselves if our moral actions might have been motivated by inclination, rather than duty. But even in this case, the point of such self-examination is not simply to judge past actions accurately, but rather to cultivate a moral disposition that takes moral obligation seriously, as opposed to thinking of it as something that is easily or even effortlessly accomplished.

Of course, rarely are motivations as simple as those described in the example. Notably, they may be mixed. But the possibility of overdetermined motives raises some difficult questions for Kant's sketch of motivation and moral worth – how should we judge an action that is seemingly motivated both by an awareness of duty and by some other inclination? One response to the puzzle has been to suggest that these motives be arranged into a kind of hierarchy.[40] In this model, an agent might be most immediately motivated by an inclination – say, fondness for a dear friend or the feeling of joy she experiences when she helps another person – but also have a kind of underlying, background motive to act from duty that ensures that these immediate motivations are kept "in line" with morality, thereby ensuring the non-contingency of moral action. In another sense, however, it may seem peculiar to discuss these cases as though the same action can have two or more motives. Another solution would be to posit that the same physical action can actually be two different actions, metaphysically speaking, each with its own motive.[41]

## 7 Autonomy and the Realm of Ends

So far, we have largely been discussing the content of the moral law. The formula of universal law and the formula of humanity are both statements of a decision procedure or permissibility test that describes the Kantian moral law. Here, we begin to consider Kant's argument for the bindingness or validity of that law. We will consider the canonical arguments for the law's bindingness in Section 8. But if we think of the argument for the validity of the moral law as a mountain range that we still have to traverse, then we might think of the discussion of the formula of autonomy and the realm of ends at the end of section two of the *Groundwork* as the foothills of that mountain range.

Perhaps because the discussion of the formula of autonomy and the realm of ends occupies a kind of transitional space between Kant's description of the moral law and his argument that we are bound by that moral law, it can sometimes be a little tricky to understand the precise nature of the argument being offered in this section. In particular, how does Kant understand autonomy? Furthermore, what is the formula of autonomy, and how is this connected to Kant's previous two formulations of the categorical imperative? What is the realm (or kingdom) of ends, and why is the notion introduced in conjunction with the discussion of autonomy, of all places?

It is helpful to make a distinction between the *formula* of autonomy and the notion of autonomy as a characteristic of *willing*. Of course, the two are closely related: let us see how this is the case. The formula of autonomy is the third

---

[40] Cf. Herman, 1993, on primary and secondary motives.    [41] Cf. Timmermann, 2007.

formulation of the moral law that Kant presents, following the formula of universal law and the formula of humanity.[42] In this sense, the formula of autonomy stands alongside these other two formulations as a statement of the content of Kant's moral principle, that is, as a statement of the decision procedure the Kantian agent ought to apply when making moral decisions. Unlike the other two, the formula of autonomy is not stated in the sort of prescriptive language that we might by now be accustomed to (i.e. "act only on that maxim ..."). Instead, it is presented more or less as a description of a type of will – specifically, "a will universally legislating through all of its maxims" (*GMS*, 4:432). However, we can restate the formula of autonomy in imperatival form as: "Act with a will that is universally legislating in all of its maxims."[43]

Note that like the other formulations of the moral law, the formula of autonomy tells us something about the will that acts for the sake of morality. The formula of universal law told us something about the type of principle (the objective determining ground) that a will acting for the sake of morality must act on, and the formula of humanity told us something about the end (the subjective determining ground) that the same will must aim at. The formula of autonomy, on the other hand, is concerned not just with the objective and subjective determining grounds of the will but also with how the moral will must itself be bound to these objective and subjective determining grounds of the will. It tells us something about the nature of the will's legislation when it acts for the sake of morality. This is why it sits at the foothills of the deduction of the moral law.

The mere notion of being subject to a law is not too difficult by itself. The harder question has to do with *why* we – or, more precisely, our wills – are subject to laws. Take, for example, a rule against littering in my town. Legally, of course, I am subject to this law by virtue of being a resident or visitor in my town. But the question here is not merely "to whom does this law apply?" It is, rather, a question that the agent asks herself: "Why does this law apply to me?" Kant thinks that there are two potential answers to the question just stated. The first is familiar: I can be subject to a law because of some interest that I have. So, in the case of rules against littering, I am subject to the law because I have an interest in being a good neighbor or citizen, because I have an interest in having

---

[42] Note that this depends on how one counts the various formulae of the categorical imperative – see footnote 2 in the Introduction to this text. Here I follow the rough categorization in Paton, 1971.

[43] One might also say, "Act as though your will were universally legislating in all of its maxims," but I think this would be misleading. Kant clearly wants us to be acting autonomously, not just acting as though we are autonomous.

a tidy neighborhood, or, of course, because I have an interest in avoiding a ticket or fine for littering.

However, this type of subjugation to a law cannot be what binds a will to the *moral* law. This is because, as we have already seen, merely having some particular end or interest cannot support willing a universal, non-contingent principle. Having an interest in following a rule is simply not up to the task when it comes to moral willing because the moral law applies universally and non-contingently. In particular, it cannot be contingent upon any particular ends that an agent may or may not have. And this is true of all sorts of interests that an agent might have – the more narrowly selfish, but altogether understandable, interest in avoiding punishment, as well as the more amiable, but nevertheless contingent, interest in being a good neighbor. Kant calls the type of subjugation to the law that relies on interest "heteronomy of the will." The slogan of the heteronomous will, as Kant puts it, is: "I ought to do something *because I want something else*" (*GMS*, 4:441).

Thus, if moral willing is possible, then there must be another way for the agent's will to be bound to the moral law. There must, in other words, be another way of explaining why she is subject to the moral law. Here is where Kant introduces the notion of autonomous willing: a will is autonomous if it is not simply *subject* to the law but also at the same time the *legislator* of that law. Such a will is subject to the law not because of an *interest* it has but because it has *given the law to itself*.[44] Nor does it give itself laws arbitrarily, since this would not be consistent with a universal and non-contingent moral principle. Rather, it gives itself the universal law of morality. Universal self-legislation is thus the second way that a will can be bound to a law. And, indeed, it is how a will *must* be bound to the moral law, since any other type of obligation would be contingent. Kant calls this "autonomy of the will."

Again, it bears repeating that Kant does not take himself to have shown that we do, in fact, have autonomous wills at this stage in his argument. That is the task for the deduction of the moral law. But, in another sense, the formula and the description of autonomy bring us much closer to a deduction because now we have a clear sense of what, precisely, a deduction has to show. In order to show that the moral law applies to us, the deduction will have to show that we are, in fact, capable of autonomous willing or universal self-legislation.

Much of the preceding discussion can be difficult to understand in the abstract, so a more concrete example might help. Alongside his other interests, Kant was fascinated by debates about education and moral education in particular. A theme that emerges repeatedly in his discussions of moral education

---

[44] See Kleingeld and Willaschek (2019) for a detailed interpretation.

has to do with the use of examples. In Kant's view, it is perfectly acceptable to provide children with examples of virtue in order to show them that virtue is possible, if not always particularly comfortable or easy. However, he thinks one must absolutely avoid holding these examples up as objects of mere emulation. The distinction between being subject to a law out of interest (heteronomy of the will) and self-legislation (autonomy of the will) helps explain Kant's conviction. To teach a child to emulate another person is at best to instill in them an interest in being like that person. Aside from being contingent, this can also backfire, since the desire to be like a person can under some circumstances generate feelings of resentment toward that person. Kant notes that telling a child to be more like Fritz next door will often cause that child to resent Fritz (VMo-Collins, 27:437). Of course, someone who has an interest in being like a good person will often act in ways that are indistinguishable from the person whose will is universally self-legislated. But there is a difference in the way they are subject to the principles they act upon, and for Kant, this makes all the difference. The former will emulate virtuous behavior so long as she has an antecedent interest in doing so; the latter will just *be virtuous*.

Finally, how does the notion of a "realm of ends" relate to Kant's discussion of autonomy and the formula of autonomy? To answer this question, we can think of the realm of ends as generalizing Kant's discussion of autonomous willing across the entire community. Specifically, every member of the realm of ends is simultaneously the legislator of the moral law and also subject to that law.

## 8 Freedom of the Will and the Deduction of Morality

So far, we have been considering the question: *If there is a moral principle, what would that principle have to be?* Typically, Kant observes, philosophers have tried to answer this question by providing an account of value and then appealing to some teleological principle in order to derive a moral principle that tells us that we ought to bring about some end or maximize some value. Kant's innovation is to reject this way of attempting to answer the question and to look instead for the answer by examining the notion of a moral law itself.

Crucially, however, none of what we have discussed so far (corresponding roughly with what Kant discusses in the first two sections of the *Groundwork*) makes any claim about the reality of this moral principle. Kant has described the content of moral obligation, but he has not yet provided an argument that there is such a thing as moral obligation. In other words, he hasn't yet provided an argument that the moral law is binding or actually applies to us. We can thus see just how important it will be for Kant to be able to provide a successful argument for the obligatoriness of the moral law. Arguing for the reality (i.e. obligatoriness) of the moral law is to provide what Kant calls a "deduction" of the moral law. A "deduction" in Kantian terms is a proof that shows the reality or the legitimacy of a concept. It is a legal term that refers to the search for a valid title on a property. So to provide a "deduction" for the moral law is to show that we can make legitimate use of the moral law, that is, that it actually applies to us.

Kant's argument for the deduction of the moral law is notoriously tricky, much debated, and clearly changes over the course of his own writings. However, the backbone of the argument is an identification between a will that is bound by the moral law and a free will. This thesis is referred to as the reciprocity thesis.[45] We can begin with that argument.

## 8.1 The Reciprocity Thesis

To understand the reciprocity thesis, it helps think about what is meant when we refer to a will that is free from deterministic influence. Kant describes the absence of deterministic influence upon a will as a kind of "negative freedom." Now, there is an important sense in which the notion of a will that is free *only* in this way is incoherent for Kant. A will, as opposed to mere action, is the type of thing that has to operate according to the representation of a principle. Specifically, as we have already seen, a will has to act on the representation of some law or principle. A will subject to determinism is easy enough to understand, since causal forces provide the will with an end that prompts the use of the hypothetical imperative. But what about a will that is not determined in this way? A will that is merely free from deterministic causation would be a will that acts randomly, as it were, and this would be no *will* at all. Kant calls this sort of will an *"unding"* – literally a "non-thing," a contradiction in terms. A will that is free must also be guided by some principle. And, as we have seen, there are really only two candidates for a principle that can serve as the objective determining ground for the will – hypothetical imperatives and the categorical imperative. The hypothetical imperative serves as the principle of willing when it comes to the action that is prompted by external influence (desire and inclination). By elimination, then, the categorical imperative, or the moral law, must be the principle that guides a free will. Kant even sometimes refers to the moral law as the causal law of a free will. A free will is thus a will that is guided (or indeed "caused") by the moral law. It is also the case that any will bound by the moral law will have to be a will that is free from causal determinism. Putting these two observations together, we arrive at the so-called reciprocity thesis: a will bound by the moral law is a free will, and a free will must

---

[45] See Allison, 1990.

be a will that is also bound by the moral law. Or, in more precise terms, a will that is free and a will that is bound by the moral law are one and the same.

The reciprocity thesis is a major clue to the puzzle of showing that we are, in fact, bound by the moral law. Having established the reciprocity thesis, Kant will be able to show that the moral law applies necessarily to any will that is free. Kant's task, at least in the *Groundwork*, thus becomes the task of showing that our wills are free. This is no small task for any philosopher, but it is a particular challenge for Kant, since he has argued in the *Critique of Pure Reason* that the freedom of the will is something that cannot be proven via theoretical reason – that is, either through empirical observation and study or through nonempirical argumentation. If Kant is to show that rational beings have wills that are free in the way described above, he will have to approach the question from the standpoint of practical reason – that is, reasoning about action. The third section of the *Groundwork* is largely devoted to offering such an argument. Kant seems to make several attempts at an argument, and commentators engage in a lively discussion about these attempts – how many there are, and whether the arguments are even remotely successful. Here, we will focus on three candidates.

## 8.2 Acting under the Idea of Freedom

The first argument that Kant seems to offer in favor of freedom runs as follows:

> ... every being that cannot act otherwise than under the idea of freedom is actually free, in a practical respect, precisely because of that, i.e. all laws that are inseparably bound up with freedom hold for it just as if its will had also been declared free in itself, and in a way that is valid in theoretical philosophy. (*GMS*, 4:448)

Kant concludes that we must "lend ... the idea of freedom" to any rational being who acts under the idea of freedom in this way. The argument, such as it is, appears to move from an observation about intentional action – or how we conceive of intentional action – to a conclusion about the nature of the will. But Kant underscores the limitations of this sort of argument: he is not offering a theoretical proof for freedom of the will. Kant is merely "assuming" freedom in this practical respect on the basis of the fact that rational beings act under the idea of freedom (*GMS*, 4:448n). He emphasizes the provisional nature of the argument when he says that we must "lend" the idea of freedom to anyone who acts under the idea of freedom.

So what does it mean to "act under the idea of freedom"? Let us consider two interpretations of this phrase. On one account, we act under the idea of freedom whenever we act, whether this is for the sake of morality or for the sake of nonmoral ends. Take, for example, your decision to read this paragraph today. From a theoretical perspective, it is possible to understand and account for your action purely deterministically. But this is probably not how *you* thought of your action when you decided to start reading. You thought of the action as the product of a free choice. In other words, you were acting under the idea of freedom. So one way of interpreting Kant's claim is to take him to be saying that whenever we take ourselves to be acting freely, we should assume or "lend" ourselves the idea of freedom.

On another reading of the passage, the notion of the "idea of freedom" is a much narrower one, referring not to any kind of action (e.g. opening a book) but specifically to moral action. This interpretation is recommended by the fact that Kant has a technical sense of the term "idea" in his philosophical texts. Briefly, Kant thinks that a sometimes bothersome feature of human reason is that it has the ability to ask questions that it cannot answer using theoretical reason. Among these are questions about the nature of our wills (whether they are free), the existence of a deity, and the nature of the soul, in particular, whether it is immortal. Although we cannot answer these questions using theoretical reason (i.e. we cannot answer these questions through any combination of empirical observation and metaphysical argumentation), Kant thinks we may be able to answer them via practical reason. An "idea of reason," in Kantian terminology, is one of these "ideas" that can only be proved via practical reason, specifically moral reasoning. If we take Kant to be using the term "idea" in this narrower sense, then "acting under the idea of freedom" would describe moral action or acting autonomously.

Neither interpretation of "acting under the idea of freedom" yields a successful argument, however. Kant realizes this almost immediately; despite even the cautious and provisional nature of the argument, he backs away from it, worrying that he has argued in a kind of a circle (*GMS*, 4:450). Why is the argument circular? Assuming the first interpretation of "acting under the idea of freedom," Kant isn't arguing in a circle as much as he is helping himself to unwarranted premises. Indeed, Kant refers to the mistake he may be making as a "*petitio principii*," a fallacy in which one assumes a premise that one is not entitled to assume.[46] On this interpretation, what Kant seems to realize is that lending oneself the idea of freedom won't suffice when it comes to the argumentative aims that he has, namely, showing that rational agents actually *are* bound or obligated by the moral law. There may be a sense in which the notion of lending ourselves the idea of freedom makes sense as a best-effort solution to the metaphysical problem of determinism, considered from the first-personal

---

[46] *GMS*, 4:453. See also Allison, 2011.

perspective. This strategy might help an agent make sense of her actions in a world that seems otherwise causally determined. But the approach won't do when it comes to providing the crucial premise in the deduction of morality. For that argument to succeed, Kant has to show that rational beings *are* free, not simply that they can assume freedom in a practical respect or that we can lend to them the idea of freedom.

If, on the other hand, Kant means to refer to moral freedom (i.e. autonomy) when he refers to the "idea of freedom," the argument does not fall prey to quite the same problem, but it is more obviously circular. On the narrower, purely moral, understanding of "acting under the idea of freedom," Kant is not referring to an action that seems free but to action that is actually free. We have already seen this connection between morality and freedom in the reciprocity thesis and in Kant's understanding of an autonomous will. But, of course, Kant cannot legitimately appeal to this sense of freedom without assuming the legitimacy of the moral law. But that is precisely what he had set out to prove the validity of in the first place. Kant could easily prove the validity of the moral law via this narrower sense of freedom, but alas, it appears he has no way of proving this narrower sense of freedom without appealing to the moral law. Kant needs to find a way out of this circle.

## 8.3 Inhabiting Two Worlds

Kant's way out of the circle will be to appeal to a distinction between the world of sense and appearance and a world that lies beyond sense and appearance. This distinction requires the introduction of some new Kantian terminology; nevertheless, Kant thinks the argument he provides rests upon largely commonsensical premises.

First, Kant observes that even the "commonest understanding" must concede a distinction between objects as we experience them and the way that those objects might really be or, in Kantian terminology, how they might be "in themselves" (*GMS*, 4:450–451). Given that Kant thinks this first observation is largely commonsensical – he also thinks it requires "no subtle thinking" – it seems unlikely that it contains the detailed metaphysical and epistemological apparatus of his critical theoretical philosophy, as described in the *Critique of Pure Reason* and the *Prolegomena*, for example. Instead, I think we can take Kant to be making a more general idealist point that there is no reason to think that the way we experience things is the way that those things are in themselves.

Once we concede this point, Kant thinks "that one must concede and assume behind the appearances something else that is not appearance, namely, the things in themselves" (*GMS*, 4:451). Kant is at this stage appealing to a distinction central to his theoretical philosophy between a world of appearance and a world that lies beyond appearance that is nevertheless the basis of appearance. The former is often referred to as the "phenomenal" world or the "world of sense"; the latter is often referred to as the "noumenal" world, the "world of understanding" or the "intellectual" or "intelligible world" depending on the context. One might reasonably wonder if one *has* to concede this distinction, assuming that one grants the commonsensical starting observation. It bears keeping in mind, though, that Kant makes what is for him a rather general point about the world of sense and the world of understanding, that is, that the latter is the basis of the former. He is not at this stage insisting that his reader accept any particular thesis about the world of understanding – that is, that it is nontemporal or nonspatial or that it is in some other way very different from the world of sense. Here, Kant only wants his reader to accept a distinction between the world as she experiences it and a world that lies behind and beyond that experience.

Next, Kant thinks that we must concede this distinction between the sensible and the intelligible even when we turn reflection inward and think about ourselves. Most of what we know about ourselves comes from the inner sense, but from the sense nonetheless. I feel pangs of hunger or jolts of happiness; I remember moments of sadness and reflect on how I came to know things. All of this belongs to the inner sense. Still, Kant thinks, just as in the outer world, we must concede that there is something that lies beyond and at the basis of all of these inner observations, and this is the "I." What Kant hopes to have shown at this stage of the argument is that we have two "selves" – the self that belongs to the world of sense that we come to know about via inner sense (and sometimes through outer sense, as when a trusted friend tells us that we have a bad habit) and the self that belongs to the intellectual world. Again, Kant is not asking that we commit to any particular picture of the latter self, just that the distinction exists.

Once Kant has the distinction between the two selves in place, he can examine each in more detail. Of course, we are very familiar with the first self – the self that we come to know via inner sense. This is the self that feels hunger or thirst and sets out to quench those feelings. It is the self that has feelings and desires and acts on the basis of these. But what of the self that belongs to the intellectual world? How can we come to know anything about this self if it is, by definition, inaccessible to us? Fortunately, Kant thinks, it is not entirely inaccessible because when we turn our attention inward and reflect on all of the preceding, we see that we have a capacity "by which we are distinguished from all other things, even from [ourselves]" (*GMS*, 4:452) and this is reason. Reason is also the capacity through which we are able to make the distinctions outlined here – those between the world of sense and the world of understanding, between the empirical self and the intellectual self.[47]

Crucially, reason is a wholly spontaneous capacity. We have other capacities that are almost completely passive – for example, the capacity to be affected by stimuli. We also have capacities that are to some extent spontaneous, but that nevertheless rely on some passive stimulus – here Kant has in mind our capacity to organize stimuli into conceptual frameworks. Reason, on the other hand, is totally spontaneous. So now we know something about our intelligible self: it is a spontaneous self of reason. As such, Kant concludes, "a human being can never think of the causality of his own will otherwise than under the idea of freedom" (*GMS*, 4:452). The causality of our empirical self is, of course, natural determinism. When I feel hunger, I eat and then no longer feel hunger. But our intellectual self is wholly spontaneous and free from such natural determinism. It can only think of its causality under the idea of freedom.

As we have seen, mere negative freedom is incomplete, as far as Kant is concerned. So the freedom of our intellectual self must have its own kind of causality, and this is what connects the intellectual self with autonomy. Since the causality of our intellectual self is the causality of freedom, we know (via the reciprocity thesis) that the law of our spontaneous self, belonging to the intellectual world, must be the moral law. Furthermore, since our intellectual self is the basis or ground of the empirical self, there is a sense in which its legislation has priority and applies to the will in general. It is not the case, in other words, that we have two "selves," each with its own sort of causality and legislation, constantly and arbitrarily vying for precedence. We surely experience moral struggle as a kind of conflict, but this is not a conflict between two equally situated kinds of legislation. Rather, autonomous legislation is legislation for the will in general, and it finds itself constantly challenged by the empirical self. This, notably, is why much of our moral struggle takes the form of *rationalization*. When we rationalize our actions, we try to "dress up" actions that would otherwise violate the law of autonomy as actions or maxims that correspond to it.

---

[47] It is worth noting that there is a narrower interpretation of reason's special capacity in this passage. Kant points out that "reason *under the name of the ideas* shows a spontaneity so pure" that it goes beyond the limited spontaneity of the understanding (author's emphasis). It could, then, be the case that reason shows its spontaneity when it considers the "ideas" discussed above – moral freedom, God, and the immortality of the soul. In this case, we may worry that he has introduced another circle in his attempt to escape the previous one, since the argument would rely, potentially, on reason's grasp of autonomous freedom. Alternately, this interpretation might suggest that Kant already had in mind the argument offered later in the *Critique of Practical Reason*, discussed in Section 8.4.

Kant thus concludes:

> [T]hus categorical imperatives are possible, because the idea of freedom makes me a member of an intelligible world, in virtue of which, if I were that alone, all my actions *would* always conform with the autonomy of the will, but as at the same time I intuit myself as a member of the world of sense, they *ought* to conform with it. (*GMS*, 4:454)

As he notes here, one interesting result of the preceding is that if we only had an intellectual self, all of our actions would automatically conform with autonomy of the will. This, roughly, is Kant's sketch of a theoretical placeholder that he calls a "holy will." But of course, we are not just our intellectual selves; we occupy two worlds. We thus experience morality not as the automatic determination of our will but as an obligation or imperative. Because our wills are pulled away from autonomous willing by inclination and desire, we experience morality as an "ought" and as a kind of struggle or, indeed, sacrifice.

To what extent does Kant succeed in his argumentative aims? To what extent does Kant succeed in showing that we are, in fact, bound by the moral law? Even on the most charitable interpretation of Kant's argument, the results are mixed. In one sense, Kant has ostensibly succeeded in providing a deduction – that is, proof of title – of the moral law. By showing that the moral law is the law of a purely spontaneous, rational self, Kant has shown that the moral law is not a mere chimera or fiction. It is the law that applies to a rational will grounded in a spontaneous, intellectual self. Insofar as we take Kant to have shown that we have a spontaneous, intellectual self, the deduction yields a description of the kind of law that is legislative for us and that argument probably succeeds.

If, however, the question of the deduction is a first-personal, agential question – "why should **I** follow the moral law?" – the argument thus far appears to be less successful. Recall that we experience morality as an imperative, as an "ought." We can think, perhaps, of Kant as having shown that the voice of this "ought" is not a mere chimera or fiction. But what he has not yet shown is why, when the chips are down and inclination has spoken, we should *listen* to this "ought." Why should we be *moved to follow* the law of autonomy that yields this imperative? Again, this is not a difficult question for purely intellectual "holy wills." For them, the motivational question just is the descriptive question. Or, more precisely, the motivational question does not pose itself in the first place because sensibility never provides any counter-suggestion to autonomy. But for us, existing as we do between nature and freedom, the motivational question remains a puzzle. In order to see a potential solution, we turn to the scoundrel and the fact of reason.

## 8.4 The Scoundrel, the Fact of Reason, and the Gallows

In the preface to the *Groundwork of the Metaphysics of Morals*, Kant explains that he will begin his investigation by examining common sense judgments, particularly those regarding moral worth; he also notes that he will return to common sense at the end of the book. With his discussion of the "scoundrel" in the final section of the book, Kant makes good on this promise. Referring to the argument surveyed above, Kant remarks:

> The practical use of common human reason confirms the correctness of this deduction. There is no one, not even the most hardened scoundrel, if only he is in the habit of using reason, who – when one presents him with examples of probity and purpose, of steadfastness in following good maxims, of compassion and of general benevolence (involving in addition great sacrifices of advantages and comfort) – does not wish that he too might be so disposed.
>
> (*GMS,* 4:454)

Even "the most hardened scoundrel" wishes he, too, could be moved by the moral law when he reflects on examples of virtue. He is kept from fulfilling this wish in himself by his own inclinations. Nevertheless, the wish to "be so disposed" shows something important in its own right. In wishing, despite his inclination, to be more like the example of morality before him, he "transfers himself in thought" to the world of understanding.

The example of the scoundrel is meant to confirm the deduction of morality that immediately precedes it. The scoundrel's wish proves that he occupies both the world of sense and the world of understanding and that he is, perhaps, more at home in the latter, even if his inclinations keep him from it. But it is probably more accurate to say that the "scoundrel" passage marks an attempt at a new type of argument for Kant, both in the method of argumentation and its ultimate conclusion. Kant still relies on the reciprocity thesis, but now he seems to argue that we can confirm our membership in the world of understanding (and thereby our freedom) via the fact that morality seems to have a kind of pull on us. Or, in other words, Kant's argument now seems to begin by appealing to precisely what was missing in the earlier deduction: the first-personal "pull" of the moral law.[48]

And, indeed, in his later work, the *Critique of Practical Reason*, Kant seems clearly to favor precisely this approach. There, he reiterates the reciprocity thesis that "freedom and unconditional practical law reciprocally imply one

---

[48] Alternatively, the scoundrel passage might suggest that elements of Kant's later argument are already present in the *Groundwork* (see also the remark in footnote 46). For discussion of whether Kant's argument changes significantly between the two texts, see Timmermann, 2010 and Ware, 2017.

another" (*KpV*, 5:29). Now, however, he explicitly denies that the previous strategy – of trying to show that we are bound by the unconditional practical law because we are free – is at all possible (*KpV*, 5:30). Instead, he argues that we acquire practical knowledge of our freedom because we are, undeniably, bound by the moral law. In a passage that is perhaps as puzzling as it is important, Kant asserts that consciousness of the moral law is a "fact of reason": we are immediately aware of it, and it "forces itself upon us as a synthetic a priori proposition."[49]

Kant is aware of how odd this might all sound: he acknowledges after a description of the pure, autonomous will that "the thing is strange enough."[50] Of course, there is not much Kant can do to argue for the fact of reason, since it asserts itself as an immediate awareness and is not derivable from prior premises or experience. Kant's ultimate claim is that a little reflection will reveal that – like the scoundrel – we are already committed, however imperfectly, to the universal practical principle of morality. Though he cannot exactly argue for this point, he can attempt to demonstrate it. And this is what he sets out to do in a famous passage about a person facing the threat of execution under two very different circumstances.

Kant first asks us to imagine a person with a seemingly irresistible lustful inclination and the opportunity to satisfy this inclination. But now suppose that we erect a gallows in front of the house where he plans on satisfying his inclination and tell him that he will be hanged "immediately after gratifying his lust" (*KpV*, 5:30). Kant predicts that the inclination that just moments ago seemed irresistible will no longer determine the agent's action. Though he might feel disappointed that he cannot satisfy his lustful inclination without bringing about his own demise, he will nevertheless choose the course of action that best furthers his own happiness, in this case avoiding temptation in order to avoid execution.

Kant now asks us to consider a different scenario. Instead of being faced with a choice about whether to satisfy his lustful inclination, our agent is faced with a different type of choice. In this case, a prince has asked him to give "false testimony against an honest man whom the prince would like to destroy under a plausible pretext." If he does not comply, the prince will execute him. Kant observes that in this case, our agent "would consider it possible to overcome his love of life, however great it may be. He would perhaps not venture to assert whether he would do it or not, but he must admit without hesitation that it would

---

[49] In Kant's terminology, consciousness of the moral law is a "*Tat der Vernunft*," which might equally be translated "deed of reason." On this point and further interpretative questions surrounding the fact of reason, see Kleingeld, 2010.

[50] Cf. Uleman, 2010.

be possible for him" (*KpV*, 5:30). The two cases have surface-level similarities: in both, the agent is faced with a choice and the threat of execution. Beyond this, however, they could not be more different. In the first scenario, the agent will automatically choose whatever brings about the most pleasure (where this also includes avoiding displeasure). In the second case, there is a question about what he will do, and this makes all the difference. When we are faced with a moral question, empirical practical reason competes with pure practical reason. This, as we have already seen, manifests as a sense of obligation. Kant accepts that many of us would ultimately fall prey to moral weakness. Nevertheless, we recognize what we *could* do because we recognize what we *should*, morally, do.

## 8.5 *Wille, Willkür,* and "Reasons" to be Moral

Before drawing this section to a close, it is worth pausing to note an apparent problem with Kant's identification of a free will and a will bound by the moral law, as described in the reciprocity thesis.[51] The worry is as follows: if a free will and a will bound by the moral law are one and the same, then it would seem that we are only free when we are bound by the moral law, that is, when we act morally from the motive of duty. Conversely and perhaps even more problematically, it would seem that we are not free when we fail to act morally, since then the empirical causal law is the determining ground of our will and not the free, self-legislated, and universal principle of morality. In sum, the reciprocity thesis would seem to suggest that we are free and thus morally responsible for our actions only when we act morally; conversely, that when we fail to act morally, we are not free and thus not morally responsible for our failure.

Kant notices this problem, perhaps even earlier than his critics realize.[52] His answer to the objection is to point to a distinction between *Wille* (usually translated simply as "will") and *Willkür* ("power of choice") (*MS*, 6:226–227). As we have already noted, our will (*Wille*) can be guided or determined either by hypothetical imperatives or the categorical imperative. We can, in other words, have a heteronomous will or an autonomous will (*Wille*). In a sense, of course, this only explains moral and nonmoral action in terms of their principles. Fundamentally, we must also make a *choice* between heteronomy and autonomy, and this is the task of our elective power of choice (*Willkür*). Kant often describes this choice with the metaphor of a crossroads (e.g. *GMS*, 4:440). Sometimes, he will also describe it as a fundamental choice of

---

[51] The objection famously appears in Reinholt, 1792/2005 and Sidgwick, 1874.
[52] Cf. *VMo-Powalski*, 27:140 and the discussion in Timmermann, 2018b.

subordination and prioritization: we choose, fundamentally, to subordinate self-love (heteronomy) to the moral law (autonomy), or vice versa (*R*, 6:36).

The notion of *Willkür* is difficult and a little mysterious, to be sure. Importantly, however, it also helps explain why appealing to "reasons" – in the sense of having a reason to act morally – is anathema for Kant. Reasons, in this sense, are surely coherent insofar as we are talking about the ends that our will (*Wille*) sets for itself, along with the corresponding principle that it acts upon. In the case of nonmoral action, the fact that I am thirsty can be a descriptive reason for my pouring myself a glass of water. When it comes to morality, there is a different, and more limited, sense in which we might appeal to humanity in ourselves or others as a kind of reason to act in a certain way, *assuming the elective power of choice (Willkür) has already endorsed or accepted the moral law as binding.* Insofar, however, as we appeal to reasons in response to the skeptical, "why be moral" question, we have introduced heteronomy into the moral system.

Of course, without being able to appeal to reasons, the choice to be moral, or to act autonomously, may seem arbitrary. In a sense, it *is and must be* arbitrary, in the sense of being inexplicable, precisely because if we appealed to some other end or principle to justify morality, then it would no longer be *morality*, at least as far as Kant would recognize it. But *Willkür* needn't thus be arbitrary in the sense of being capricious or random. Indeed, what Kant intends to show via the fact of reason and the gallows passage is that the fundamental choice to be moral is not random at all but, expressive of our very rational nature.

## 9 Common Objections to Kant's Ethics

Having surveyed some of Kant's foundational arguments regarding the content of the moral law and the nature of moral obligation, we are in a good position to consider some of the more common objections to Kantian ethics. Few of these objections are new: many of them have an ancestor in reviews and other texts that appeared almost immediately after the publication of the *Groundwork*. Often, these criticisms rest on a misunderstanding of Kant's moral framework; it can thus be useful to consider these misunderstandings to get a better grasp of Kant's arguments. Sometimes, these objections rest less on a misunderstanding regarding Kant's foundational arguments and more on a worry about the implications of Kant's view – for example, that it is cold, unsympathetic, or overly demanding. In these cases, it is worth considering to what extent these implications really do follow from Kant's foundational arguments.

## 9.1 Kantian Morality Is Excessively Rational

Given the preeminence of universality and rationality in Kant's moral system, it is not altogether surprising that commentators often take Kantian ethics to be excessively rational – perhaps even to the point of absurdity or emptiness. There are at least two forms that this criticism can take: The first of these is that Kant's decision procedure, as described by the formula of universal law, is contentless and presents an "empty formalism," to cite Hegel's famous criticism.[53] The second is the skeptical worry – considered briefly previously – that merely noticing that our maxim is not universalizable cannot possibly compel me to avoid that action, that is, it does nothing to prove to me that I have some obligation to avoid that action, morally.

First, let us consider the worry that Kant's ethics presents a kind of empty formalism. We can think of this objection in terms of a kind of dilemma for Kant. In the first instance, it seems that the categorical imperative (the formula of universal law), cannot, by itself, yield any concrete moral advice, since it is a purely formal test. Indeed – so the criticism goes – in order to get the test to offer any results in the form of moral prohibitions or suggestions, we have to input all kinds of empirical data – for example, about our inclinations or about the nature of human beings. But if we can say anything about Kant's arguments regarding the foundations of morality, it is that they insist on universality and necessity and thus cannot rest on empirical facts. So we seem to have a dilemma: either Kant's famous moral principle is empty or it secretly (or not-so-secretly) violates the standards of Kant's system by appealing to and relying upon empirical data.

Kant would have no argument with the first horn of the dilemma. After all, as we have seen (Section 4), he himself takes the categorical imperative to be a purely formal (i.e. nonmaterial) practical principle. Anything else would fail to describe a necessary and universal moral principle. Thus, the response to the objection is to consider carefully the second horn of the dilemma. In what sense does Kant's system rely upon or appeal to empirical facts? And is this as problematic as the objection makes it out to be?

There are two ways that the formula of universal law takes empirical data into account, but neither of these is problematic from the standpoint of Kant's stated aims. First, recall that the categorical imperative, as a test or decision procedure, needs *something to test*, and these will be the maxims that agents form on the basis of desire and inclination. Crucially, as we have already noted, inclination always gets the first word, or the first move, in the conversation between sensibility and morality. Once we have formed a maxim on the basis of

---

[53] Hegel, 1803/1975, but the objection is already raised by Tittel, 1786.

inclination and empirical deliberation, only then can we test our maxim against the formula of universal law or another formulation of the categorical impera- tive, in order to see if it is universalizable. This, however, does not undermine the nonempirical nature of the categorical imperative *itself*. It would, of course, be a different matter entirely if the inclinations and desires that contribute to maxim-formation were somehow embedded in the principle itself – for example, if the principle recommended pursuing as many of one's own maxims as possible.

Of course, empirical facts about the world and the nature of human beings are arguably even more important to the tests that produce contradictions in willing and thus generate facts about imperfect duty. Take, for example, the test that generates the imperfect duty of beneficence: there the contradiction only arises because the agent recognizes that she is a finite creature who also needs the assistance of others – thus generating a contradiction between her own will and the universalized maxim of non-beneficence. However, even in this case, the principle of morality – to act only on a maxim that one could also will as a universal law – remains free of any empirical component.

A second objection regarding Kant's alleged rationalism centers not on the feasibility of the categorical imperative as a nonempirical test of morality, but on whether such a test could actually yield obligation. The objection, in other words, is that even if the categorical imperative can generate contradictions between my maxim and a universalized maxim, the mere fact of this contradic- tion cannot possibly generate an obligation or convince me that I have a duty to refrain from acting according to my maxim. The reply to this objection, as we have seen throughout, is that Kant never intends for the categorical imperative to serve as an argument for moral obligation. It is only the statement of a moral law that finds its ultimate deduction or proof in Kant's arguments regarding the will (Section 8).[54]

## 9.2 Kantian Motivation Is Fetishistic

A related worry is that Kant's ethics is, to put it perhaps tendentiously, fetishis- tic. Previously (Section 2), we briefly considered the worry that Kant's ethics demands a kind of obsessive and absolutist rule-following, and we saw that this is a misrepresentation of Kant's ethics, since Kant does not offer a system of

---

[54] An objection related to these concerns about hyper-rationality is that Kant's ethics makes no room for nonhuman animals or human beings who are not fully rational, including children. As noted in Section 3, Kant's theory commits him to the view that morality cannot obligate nonrational humans or nonhuman animals. However, there is room to argue that we still have duties with regard to such beings. See Kain, 2010; Korsgaard, 2018; Timmermann, 2005; and Varden, 2020.

rules, but rather a test of permissibility.[55] But beyond this worry, there may be a further concern prompted by the observation that Kantian agents ought, apparently, to be motivated by the sheer fact that something is commanded by duty. But this seems both an inaccurate and unpleasant description of moral action – surely we sometimes act for the sake of things like friendship and loyalty when we act morally.

The source of this objection, as we have seen, lies in Kant's rejection of an empirical or teleological account of the ground of moral action. In other words, Kant rejects any ethical system that locates the source of goodness in some end or value that ought to be pursued or maximized. However, in rejecting these, Kant also denies himself an easy account of moral motivation. A utilitarian who seeks to maximize happiness can be plausibly motivated by the prospect of achieving more general happiness, in its many forms; a Kantian must, somehow, be motivated by the thought or recognition of duty itself.

Much of the force of this objection, I suspect, comes from one of two misunderstandings. The first is a worry that Kant is suggesting that we judge all actions – our own and those of others – according to this rubric. But, as we have seen, this is largely a misunderstanding of Kant's aims in his discussion of moral worth, especially in the first section of the *Groundwork*. It is unquestionably true, for Kant, that actions performed from the motive of duty have a kind of moral worth that actions performed for the sake of inclination do not. But this does not mean that actions performed for the sake of inclination – especially those performed for the sake of immediate inclination – are *bad or immoral*. It simply means that moral action cannot be motivated by those inclinations. Still, less does Kant think that we ought to judge others according to what we think their motivating grounds are. We may have some reason to interrogate our *own* motivations in this way, as a way of fostering a virtuous disposition and lowering our general resistance to morality, but it is a misunderstanding of Kant's aims to think that questions of right and wrong correspond to questions of moral motivation or that agents ought to be concerned with interrogating the motivations of others in order to make moral judgments.

A second mistake, it seems, is to think that Kantian agents ought to act for the sake of duty just for the sake of acting from duty as if they were compelled to follow rules just for the sake of following rules. This worry rests on a misunderstanding that is not too far removed from the misunderstanding

---

[55] An objection often raised in this regard is that Kant's ethics seems to require a person to tell the truth to the proverbial murderer at the door, who is intent on killing a friend hiding in the house. An adequate Kantian response to the objection is beyond the scope of this text, since it also requires a discussion of Kant's legal philosophy. Mahon (2009) offers an excellent overview of the ethical and juridical (legal) senses of lying in Kant.

that looks for an account of obligation in the formula of universal law itself. Kant does not expect us to act from duty in some particular case because the categorical imperative tells us that a certain maxim is impermissible. We act from duty because this is the way we act when we are free and not determined by sensibility. Now, of course, this response might not always be open to a Kantian who wants to avoid such metaphysical territory. Even so, however, it is a misnomer to say that Kantian agents act – or ought to act – *just* for the sake of duty. After all, Kant's moral theory does have an account of value, albeit not the kind of value that can or should be pursued in consequentialist terms. For Kant, value is determined by the law, not vice versa. Still, when an agent acts from duty, she also acts to preserve or promote humanity in herself or another. What is more, all sorts of more familiar moral motivations can often be subsumed under this description. Take, for example, an agent who acts out of friendship. In a sense, acting merely out of "friendship" is as abstract and potentially contentless as acting merely out of duty. "Acting out of friendship," I suspect, is more or less shorthand for a number of considerations that square perfectly well with treating another person as an end in herself. When we act out of friendship or loyalty, we act on the basis of commitments specific to the relationship, commitments that have developed over a period of close associ- ation and through fondness for one another. Nevertheless, I would argue, these are fundamental commitments to or regarding the humanity in another person, not just to our friend qua friend.[56]

## 9.3 Kantian Motivation Admits of No Room for Feeling

A byproduct, perhaps, of the singular emphasis on acting from duty mentioned above is the worry that Kantian ethics is "cold and calculating" and admits of no room for feeling, particularly in its account of moral motivation. This is potentially problematic for at least two reasons. First, it is difficult to make sense of an account of moral motivation that doesn't have at least some role for desire or feeling. Second, it may make Kant's account of moral action unpalat- able, especially when it comes to close, interpersonal moral interactions.

Of course, as we have already seen, Kant's account of acting from duty does not exclude feeling altogether. In particular, Kant posits a type of feeling that is specific to moral motivation, namely, the feeling of respect. The difference between the feeling of respect and other feelings that might ultimately motiv- ate us, for example, by developing into inclinations and, ultimately, ends, is that the feeling of respect is not passively received like the so-called patho- logical feelings are. Instead, Kant says, the feeling of respect is a feeling that is

---

[56] This claim is similar to one advanced by Velleman, 1999.

"self-wrought by a rational concept" (*GMS*, 4:401n). In the *Critique of Practical Reason*, Kant gives some more details regarding how this feeling comes about: notably, it is a feeling that only emerges once we experience a kind of pain that results from having some of our self-interested ends thwarted by morality. Once we experience this kind of pain or humiliation, Kant notes, we can also develop a kind of awe or reverence for the moral law that thwarted or struck down our initial ends (*KpV*, 5:73). Notably, Kant also lists a number of so-called aesthetic preconditions for the functioning moral agent in the *Doctrine of Virtue* (*MS*, 6:399); these sensuous requirements include moral feeling, conscience, love (of others), and self-respect.

So it is clear that feeling is not altogether absent from Kant's account of morality. Still less does Kant think that the ideal agent would somehow be completely unfeeling or robotic in her performance of duty. Nevertheless, respect for the moral law is a unique type of feeling: it is not like love, friendship, joy, or sadness because it is not passively received but spontaneously generated, as a result of our active engagement, as it were, with the moral law. This observation brings us to the second set of concerns about the role that Kant allows for feeling when it comes to moral motivation. In particular, Kant's account of respect for the moral law will not satisfy the critic who thinks that at least in some cases, feelings like love and care for others should actually be what motivates us. Often, this sort of objection asks the reader to imagine what it would be like to interact with a Kantian who acts only out of duty, especially if that Kantian happens to be a friend, spouse, or some other such person of whom we hope or expect love and affection.[57]

The Kantian literature that aims to put this sort of critic at ease is vast, and one could hardly do it justice here.[58] Still, a few observations are worth emphasizing. First, these sorts of criticisms often derive some of their argumentative force from the presumption that acting from duty is at odds with acting from immediate inclinations like love or friendship. But as we have already seen (Section 6), this is not true. They appear to be at odds, largely because of the way that Kant is forced to present them in order to isolate and highlight the moral motive of respect against a background of other types of motives. Nevertheless, it seems possible, at least, to be moved by motives of friendship or love while also being moved by the motive of duty.

This last observation brings us to a second assumption that, I think, often underlies these sorts of objections, namely, that if feeling like love and friendship cannot motivate moral action, then Kant's ethics is also unable to account

---

[57] Stocker, 1976 and Williams, 1981.
[58] See, for example, Baron, 1984, 1995; Guyer, 1993; Herman, 1993.

for the intuition that we have special bonds with loved ones, some of which might give rise to moral obligation. Kant's rejection of feeling, in other words, makes his moral system far *too* impartial, since it denies an important sphere of moral engagement. But, again, nothing in the Kantian framework speaks against having duties to particular people, nor does anything in the Kantian picture speak against developing relationships out of feelings like love and affection and then recognizing that those relationships imply or generate their own sets of obligations.

Fundamentally, Kant's rejection of pathological feeling as a moral motivation has to do with its contingency. And, as most of us know, even the strongest feelings of friendship, romantic love, or filial love can sometimes be mixed with resentments or annoyances that can get in the way of acting as we should toward our loved ones. This fact seems often to be overlooked in criticisms of Kant that paint him as unfriendly to feelings of love and friendship. Once we note that there is nothing about these relationships and their attendant feelings that is necessarily at odds with Kant's account of dutiful action, we can also come to see that Kantian moral commitments can themselves be a part of what it is to be a good friend, partner, or parent.

## 9.4 Kantian Ethics Is Unconcerned with Outcomes

Kant was not a consequentialist. He rejects the idea that one could derive a universal principle of morality by first identifying some contingent object of value and then setting out to bring it about or maximize it. But, we might wonder: don't consequences matter? Surely it makes a difference, morally speaking, if my actions make someone happy. Or to increase the stakes a bit: surely it makes a difference, morally speaking, if a life devoted to the pursuit of justice actually brings about a better world, in the end.

Fortunately, Kant would not deny either of these claims. But to understand the role that consequences can play within the Kantian framework, we need to make a clear distinction between the ground of moral action and the object of moral action. The ground of moral action is the principle according to which we act when we act for the sake of morality. In the terminology introduced earlier, it is the objective determining ground of a moral will. The object of moral action is the state of affairs we bring about with that action. The distinction is easiest to see when we consider imperfect duties, for example, those of beneficence, since these are duties of commission. On the Kantian account, when a person forms and acts on a charitable maxim, the ground of her action is the categorical imperative. The object of her action, however, will be the state of affairs that she hopes to bring about with her action. If she donates money to Doctors Without

Borders, the object of her action will be to provide much-needed medical care to people in other parts of the world.

It is sometimes easy to overlook this distinction between the ground and object of moral action because consequentialist moral theories do not make it; more to the point, they tend to begin from the assumption that there is little or no difference between the object of moral action and its ground and that the surest way to identify the latter is to locate the former. When an agent acts on consequentialist grounds, the principle that she acts on refers – more or less explicitly – to the end or object she intends to bring about. The very derivation of a consequentialist principle requires reference to the intended object of moral action.

The distinction between ground and object of moral willing takes on a much larger, and indeed intriguing, role in Kantian ethics in the context of his theory of the highest good.[59] We can think of the highest good as the ultimate expression or summation of the relationship between ground and object of moral willing described above. It is the greatest degree of happiness consistent with the greatest degree of virtue. There is debate among Kant scholars about whether Kant thinks that this conjunction of virtue and happiness ought to obtain within the individual agent or whether it ought to obtain within a moral community, perhaps even over the course of human history.[60] What is clear, however, is that Kant views the highest good as itself the object of moral willing (*KpV*, 5:110). In the grand scheme of things, in other words, the object that we are trying to bring about with all of our moral willing is a state of affairs in which there is as much happiness as can be, given the constraints of morality. If nothing else, Kant's theory of the highest good should serve as a reminder of an often-ignored feature of his moral theory: happiness, so long as it is consistent with morality, is a good thing. A world in which there is a virtue, but no happiness is worse than a world in which there is virtue and some happiness – assuming, of course, that this happiness has not come about through immorality.

Part of what makes Kant's account of the highest good so difficult is that he uses the idea of the highest good as a premise in different types of argument. Perhaps most notably, he uses the idea that the highest good is the necessary object of morality as a premise in an argument from practical (i.e. moral) grounds for the existence of God and the immortality of the soul. In Kant's view, the existence of God and the immortality of the soul – along with freedom of the will – are metaphysical questions that cannot be answered with theoretical

---

[59] More precisely, Kant refers to this as the highest derived good (the highest original good is God). Kant's theory of the highest good is difficult and plausibly even changes over time. The literature on it is vast, and interpretations are many. Here, I can give only the broadest of sketches.

[60] See, for example, Engstrom, 1992; Guyer, 2002; Reath, 1988.

reason, certainly not via empirical observation, but also not through metaphysical argument. Kant does think, however, that it might be possible to provide practical proof of them, and his theory of the highest good is a large part of that project.

More generally, the theory of the highest good plays an important role in bridging the gulf between freedom and nature by demonstrating the crucial role that happiness (always conditioned by morality) plays in Kant's ethics. The highest good thus also plays an important role in a number of arguments that have to do more or less with the minimal epistemic conditions for moral motivation. In particular, Kant appears to acknowledge at times that we would not be able to act from duty if we knew – or perhaps even had a strong enough suspicion – that all of our moral strivings would come to nothing.[61] The ideal of the highest good thus shows that consequences do matter, in Kant's view, even if they can never serve as the ground of moral action.

## 10 Concluding Remarks

As the preceding discussion of the highest good suggests, there is more to Kant's ethics than may initially meet the eye. Though he eschews happiness as the foundation of morality and instead insists on a moral theory with nonempirical, rational foundations, Kant is not a Stoic. Feeling and, indeed, happiness play a role in his account of morality, albeit a limited account, always conditioned by morality. Perhaps most fundamentally, however, Kant describes a moral system that places the autonomous moral agent front and center. This is not without its difficulties and puzzles, as we have seen throughout this text. Nevertheless, it is a theory that emphasizes fundamental equality among rational agents, not in terms of their ability to experience pleasure, but instead in terms of a shared dignity associated with their legislative capacity.

---

[61] Kant offers a dramatic example at *KU*, 5:452–453; see also Kleingeld, 1995.

# References

## Kantian Texts and Abbreviations

Volume, page, and line numbers refer to the Academy edition of Kant's works (Berlin: De Gruyter et al., 1900–). For the most part, translations have been adapted from the Cambridge Edition of Kant's works. English versions of Kant's writings on moral and political philosophy can be found in *Immanuel Kant: Practical Philosophy*, edited by Mary Gregor and Allen Wood (Cambridge: Cambridge University Press, 1998). For a revised version of Mary Gregor's translation of the *Groundwork of the Metaphysics of Morals*, see the German-English edition edited by Mary Gregor and Jens Timmermann (Cambridge: Cambridge University Press, 2011).

Abbreviations used for Kant's works, handwritten notes and lectures:

| | |
|---|---|
| *KU* | *Critique of the Power of Judgment* (1790) |
| *KpV* | *Critique of Practical Reason* (1788) |
| *GMS* | *Groundwork of the Metaphysics of Morals* (1785) |
| *MS* | *The Metaphysics of Morals* (1797) |
| *R* | *Religion within the Boundaries of Mere Reason* (1793) |
| VMo-Collins | Moral Philosophy Lectures Collins (1784–1785) |
| VMo-Powalski | Practical Philosophy Lectures Powalski (1782–1783) |

## Secondary Sources

Allison, H. (1990). *Kant's Theory of Freedom*. New York: Cambridge University Press.

Allison, H. (1996). On the Presumed Gap in the Derivation of the Categorical Imperative. In *Idealism and Freedom: Essays on Kant's Theoretical and Practical Philosophy*. New York: Cambridge University Press.

Allison, H. (2011). *Kant's Groundwork for the Metaphysics of Morals: A Commentary*. New York: Oxford University Press.

Aune, B. (1980). *Kant's Theory of Morals*. Princeton: Princeton University Press.

Baron, M. (1984). The Alleged Moral Repugnance of Acting from Duty. *Journal of Philosophy* 81(4): 197–220.

Baron, M. (1995). *Kantian Ethics (Almost) without Apology*. Ithaca: Cornell University Press.

Baron, M. (2008). Virtue Ethics, Kantian Ethics, and the "One Thought Too Many" Objection. In M. Betzler (ed.), *Kant's Ethics of Virtues*. Berlin: DeGruyter.

Baxley, A. (2010). *Kant's Theory of Virtue: The Value of Autocracy*. New York: Cambridge University Press.

Dean, R. (2006). *The Value of Humanity in Kant's Moral Theory*. New York: Oxford University Press.

Engstrom, S. (1992). The Concept of the Highest Good in Kant's Moral Theory. *Philosophy and Phenomenological Research* 52: 747–780.

Formosa, P. and Sticker, M. (2019). Kant and the Demandingness of the Duty of Beneficence. *European Journal of Philosophy* 27: 625–642.

Gaut, B. and Kerstein, S. (1999). The Derivation without the Gap: Rethinking Groundwork I. *Kantian Review* 3: 18–40.

Glasgow, J. (2003). Expanding the Limits of Universalization. *Canadian Journal of Philosophy* 33: 23–47.

Guyer, P. (1993). *Kant and the Experience of Freedom: Essays on Aesthetics and Morality*. New York: Cambridge University Press.

Guyer, P. (1998). The Value of Reason and the Value of Freedom. *Ethics* 109: 22–35.

Guyer, P. (2002). Ends of Reason and Ends of Nature: The Place of Teleology in Kant's Ethics. *Journal of Value Inquiry* 36: 161–186.

Guyer, P. (2007). *Kant's Groundwork for the Metaphysics of Morals: A Reader's Guide*. New York: Continuum Press.

Guyer, P. (2019). *Kant on the Rationality of Morality*. New York: Cambridge University Press.

Hegel, G. W. F. (1803/1975). *On the Scientific Ways of Treating Natural Law*. Trans. T. M. Knox. Philadelphia: University of Pennsylvania Press.

Hegel, G. W. F. (1821/1991). *Elements of the Philosophy of Right*. Trans. H. B. Nisbet, Ed. A. Wood. New York: Cambridge University Press.

Herman, B. (1993). *The Practice of Moral Judgment*. Cambridge, MA: Harvard University Press.

Hill, T. (1973). The Hypothetical Imperative. *Philosophical Review* 82: 429–450.

Hill, T. (1992). *Dignity and Practical Reason in Kant's Moral Theory*. Ithaca: Cornell University Press.

Kain, P. (2010) Duties Regarding Animals. In L. Denis (ed.) Kant's *Metaphysics of Morals*: A Critical Guide. New York: Cambridge University Press.

Kleingeld, P. (1995). What Do the Virtuous Hope For? Re-Reading Kant's Doctrine of the Highest Good. In H. Robinson (ed.), *Proceedings of the*

*Eighth International Kant Congress*. Milwaukee: Marquette University Press.

Kleingeld, P. (2010). Moral Consciousness and the "Fact of Reason." In A. Reath and J. Timmermann (eds.), *Kant's Critique of Practical Reason: A Critical Guide*. New York: Cambridge University Press.

Kleingeld, P. and Willaschek, M. (2019). Autonomy without Paradox: Kant, Self-Legislation, and the Moral Law. *Philosopher's Imprint* 19(6): 1–18.

Kohl, M. (2018). Kant's Critique of Instrumental Reason. *Pacific Philosophical Quarterly* 99: 489–516.

Korsgaard, K. (1996). *Creating the Kingdom of Ends*. New York: Cambridge University Press.

Korsgaard, K. (2018). *Fellow Creatures: Our Obligations to the Other Animals*. New York: Oxford University Press.

Langton, R. (1992). Duty and Desolation. *Philosophy* 67: 481–505.

Mahon, J. (2003). Kant on Lies, Candour, and Reticence. *Kantian Review* 7: 102–133.

Mahon, J. (2009). The Truth About Kant on Lies. In C. Martin (ed.), *The Philosophy of Deception*. New York: Oxford University Press.

Martin, A. (2006). How to Argue for the Value of Humanity. *Pacific Philosophical Quarterly* 87: 96–125.

Mill, J. S. (1867). *Utilitarianism*. London: Longmans, Green, Reader, and Dyer.

O'Neill, O. (1975). *Acting on Principle*. New York: Cambridge University Press.

Papish, L. (2018). Kant's Revised Account of the Non-Moral Imperatives of Practical Reason. *Ergo: An Open Access Journal of Philosophy* 5: 289–317.

Paton, H. J. (1971). *The Categorical Imperative: A Study in Kant's Moral Philosophy*. Philadelphia: University of Pennsylvania Press.

Pistorius, H. A. (1786). Rezension der Grundlegung zur Metaphysik der Sitten. In R. Bittner and K. Cramer (eds.), *Materialien zu Kants Kritik der praktischen Vernunft*. Frankfurt: Suhrkamp.

Prichard, H. (1912). Does Moral Philosophy Rest on a Mistake? *Mind* 21: 21–37.

Rawls, J. (1971) *A Theory of Justice*. Cambridge, MA: Harvard University Press.

Rawls, J. (1980). Kantian Constructivism in Moral Theory. *Journal of Philosophy* 77(9): 515–572.

Reath, A. (1988). Two Conceptions of the Highest Good in Kant. *Journal of the History of Philosophy* 26: 593–619.

Reinholt, K. L. (1792/2005). *Letters on the Kantian Philosophy*. Trans. J. Hebbeler, Ed. K. Ameriks. New York: Cambridge University Press.

Scanlon, T. M. (1998). *What We Owe to Each Other.* Cambridge, MA: Harvard University Press.

Schroeder, M. (2005). The Hypothetical Imperative? *Australasian Journal of Philosophy* 83: 357–372.

Sidgwick, H. (1874). *The Methods of Ethics.* Indianapolis: Hackett.

Sticker, M. (2019). A Funeral March for Those Drowning in Shallow Ponds? Imperfect Duties and Emergencies. *Kant-Studien* 110: 236–255.

Stocker, M. (1976). The Schizophrenia of Modern Ethical Theories. *The Journal of Philosophy* 73(14): 453–466.

Stohr, K. (2011). Kantian Beneficence and the Problem of Obligatory Aid. *Journal of Moral Philosophy* 8: 45–67.

Timmermann, J. (2005). When the Tail Wags the Dog: Animal Welfare and Indirect Duty in Kantian Ethics. *Kantian Review* 10: 128–149.

Timmermann, J. (2006). Value without Regress: Kant's "Formula of Humanity" Revisited. *European Journal of Philosophy* 14: 69–93.

Timmermann, J. (2007). *Kant's Groundwork of the Metaphysics of Morals: A Commentary.* New York: Cambridge University Press.

Timmermann, J. (2010). Reversal or Retreat? Kant's Deductions of Freedom and Morality. In A. Reath and J. Timmermann (eds.), *Kant's Critique of Practical Reason: A Critical Guide.* Cambridge: Cambridge University Press.

Timmermann, J. (2018a). Autonomy, Progress, and Virtue: Why Kant Has Nothing to Fear from the Demandingness Objection. *Kantian Review* 23: 379–397.

Timmermann, J. (2018b). Emerging Autonomy: Dealing with the Inadequacies of the Canon of the Critique of Pure Reason. In S. Bacin and O. Sensen (eds.), *The Emergence of Autonomy in Kant's Moral Philosophy.* New York: Cambridge University Press.

Tittel, G. A. (1786). *Über Herrn Kants Moralreform.* Frankfurt/Leipzig: Pfähler.

Uleman, J. (2010). *An Introduction to Kant's Moral Philosophy.* New York: Cambridge University Press.

Uleman, J. (2016). No King and No Torture: Kant on Suicide and Law. *Kantian Review* 21: 77–100.

Varden, H. (2020). Kant and Moral Responsibility for Animals. In L. Allais and J. Callanan (eds.), *Kant on Animals.* New York: Oxford University Press.

Velleman, J. D. (1999). Love as a Moral Emotion. *Ethics* 109: 338–374.

Ware, O. (2017). Kant's Deductions of Morality and Freedom. *Canadian Journal of Philosophy* 47: 116–147.

Williams, B. (1973). A Critique of Utilitarianism. In J. J. C. Smart and B. Williams (eds.), *Utilitarianism: For and against*. New York: Cambridge University Press.

Williams, B. (1981). Persons, Character, and Morality. In *Moral Luck: Philosophical Papers 1973–1980*. New York: Cambridge University Press.

Wood, A. (1999). *Kant's Ethical Thought*. New York: Cambridge University Press.

Wood, A. (2013). Kant on Practical Reason. In M. Timmons and S. Baiasu (eds.), *Kant on Practical Justification: Interpretative Essays*. New York: Oxford University Press.

# Acknowledgments

I am grateful to Ben Eggleston, Dale E. Miller, Jens Timmermann, and two anonymous referees for their thoughtful comments on earlier drafts of this project. I am also grateful to the Institute for Advanced Study in Greifswald, Germany, for support during the later stages of this project.

Cambridge Elements

# Ethics

## Ben Eggleston
### University of Kansas

Ben Eggleston is a professor of philosophy at the University of Kansas. He is the editor of John Stuart Mill, *Utilitarianism: With Related Remarks from Mill's Other Writings* (Hackett, 2017) and a co-editor of *Moral Theory and Climate Change: Ethical Perspectives on a Warming Planet* (Routledge, 2020), *The Cambridge Companion to Utilitarianism* (Cambridge, 2014), and *John Stuart Mill and the Art of Life* (Oxford, 2011). He is also the author of numerous articles and book chapters on various topics in ethics.

## Dale E. Miller
### Old Dominion University, Virginia

Dale E. Miller is a professor of philosophy at Old Dominion University. He is the author of *John Stuart Mill: Moral, Social and Political Thought* (Polity, 2010) and a co-editor of *Moral Theory and Climate Change: Ethical Perspectives on a Warming Planet* (Routledge, 2020), *A Companion to Mill* (Blackwell, 2017), *The Cambridge Companion to Utilitarianism* (Cambridge, 2014), *John Stuart Mill and the Art of Life* (Oxford, 2011), and *Morality, Rules, and Consequences: A Critical Reader* (Edinburgh, 2000). He is also the editor-in-chief of *Utilitas*, and the author of numerous articles and book chapters on various topics in ethics broadly construed.

## About the series

This Elements series provides an extensive overview of major figures, theories, and concepts in the field of ethics. Each entry in the series acquaints students with the main aspects of its topic while articulating the author's distinctive viewpoint in a manner that will interest researchers.

# Cambridge Elements ≡

# Ethics

## Elements in the series

Printed in the United States
by Baker & Taylor Publisher Services